Addition through Subtraction

Addition through Subtraction

Revitalizing the Established Church

Desmond Barrett

Foreword by James H. Diehl

WIPF & STOCK · Eugene, Oregon

ADDITION THROUGH SUBTRACTION
Revitalizing the Established Church

Copyright © 2022 Desmond Barrett. All rights reserved. Except for brief quotations in critical publications or reviews, no part of this book may be reproduced in any manner without prior written permission from the publisher. Write: Permissions, Wipf and Stock Publishers, 199 W. 8th Ave., Suite 3, Eugene, OR 97401.

Wipf & Stock
An Imprint of Wipf and Stock Publishers
199 W. 8th Ave., Suite 3
Eugene, OR 97401

www.wipfandstock.com

PAPERBACK ISBN: 978-1-6667-3574-1
HARDCOVER ISBN: 978-1-6667-9314-7
EBOOK ISBN: 978-1-6667-9315-4

04/01/22

Scriptures taken from the Holy Bible, New International Version®, NIV®. Copyright © 1973, 1978, 1984, 2011 by Biblica, Inc.™ Used by permission of Zondervan. All rights reserved worldwide. www.zondervan.com The "NIV" and "New International Version" are trademarks registered in the United States Patent and Trademark Office by Biblica, Inc.™

I dedicate this book to my spiritual father and mentor,
Pastor Bob Lockwood.

Contents

Foreword by James H. Diehl | ix
Prologue: Serving in the Hard Places | xi

1. Staying Focused when Difficulty Comes | 1
2. Finding God's Promises in a Season of Change | 10
3. Reestablishing the Spiritual Center | 19
4. For God's Glory | 27
5. The Community Is Waiting | 36
6. Leading to Future Victories | 44
7. Living in a Spirit of Service | 53
8. What Drives You to Help Lead the Church | 62
9. Revitalization Next Steps | 67
10. Revitalize Your Church: Revitalization Efforts | 76

Bibliography | 85

Foreword

I LEARNED EARLY IN my ministry that "churches grow on morale—not money. Get the morale up and the money—and attendance—will come." Desmond Barrett illustrates this truth over and over in his book *Addition through Subtraction: Revitalizing the Established Church*. The reality of today is that we are living in the post-COVID-19 culture. Most congregations are now smaller in number, which creates more empty space in the sanctuary. It's discouraging to the pastor, staff, and lay leaders! It's you (pastor, staff, and lay leaders) that Barrett has in mind as he wrote this book.

We are encouraged to pray, pray, pray. Get creative. Change what needs to be changed. Reenergize the rest. Look at your church through the eyes of a visitor: Your church sign. The parking lot. The foyer. The bathrooms. The sanctuary. Everything! Then use wisdom to make needed changes.

Although Desmond has the degrees behind his name, this book is not from a professor's mind but rather from a pastor's heart. He is presently the pastor of a growing, established church in today's post-COVID-19 culture in Ashland, Kentucky. You will soon note that he is a gifted communicator, but he also is a gifted encourager. In my view, "we'll pay a little extra" for some

Addition through Subtraction

encouragement in this day in which we've been called by God to be spiritual leaders.

God is still God, and sinners still need to be redeemed by Jesus Christ! Don't give in to the temptation to just "let it slide." As you read Barrett's book, pray that the Holy Spirit will fan a new flame within your heart and soul. God can—and will—help you to break through in this secular age. Be encouraged and try something new in your quest to win souls for the kingdom!

Dr. James H. Diehl
general superintendent emeritus
Church of the Nazarene

Prologue
Serving in the Hard Places

SERVING AS A PASTOR in a revitalization effort can be lonely and, at times, disappointing. No wonder thousands of pastors have walked away from their calling in search of greener pastures or have left ministry altogether. Countless pastors have asked themselves in these defining moments of their ministry, "Does God, or anyone, care?" Thankfully, he does, or thousands of churches would close annually without the faithful leadership of an under-shepherd who is willing to serve in the hard places. Revitalizing the established church is about caring about the calling, coming to terms with where God has placed you, celebrating the success, and committing to continuing to move forward. It is also about understanding that subtraction takes place to add new people, programs, and passions in the future. Serving in the hard places is all about serving faithfully for God.

Serving in an established church that is struggling can make a pastor feel empty, isolated, and alone, even when others are around. The once-massive structure called the established church sits predominantly empty each Sunday except for a few sprinkled souls here and there. Once, many families entered her foyer. Today, she is a vast monument to her past growth which has become a confining coffin waiting for the pastor to speak her eulogy. One cannot underestimate the isolating effect of a small, struggling church on the pastor's psyche. As the leader walks the halls of the church, in the emptiness of the church edifice there are whispers of

Addition through Subtraction

past triumphs that seem all too much for the tragedy taking place in the dying church today. Amid the downcast aloneness of the pastor's inner being, God begins to speak to the soul of the under-shepherd to lead the church forward.

Others have left her or even mocked her, but the revitalization pastor sees—senses, really—the beauty of what God is doing. With a mighty remnant of believers, God is calling the church back to life. The shepherd of this flock must care more about the calling and the assignment than the numbers in the pews. God has called the pastor to this place and time to lead the struggling church, and if the pastor does not care, then why should the people? It will take time and "tactical patience," as Mark Clifton loves to say,[1] but she will come back alive if the pastor is willing to do the work to help her rebound from decline. While the world outside her walls ignores and might even forget she still exists, the church of Jesus Christ is still very much alive. While the location of the church does not matter to the neighbors, the address of the declining church still matters to God. Through the faithfulness of her leadership, it will matter again to the community around her. Pause and think for a moment. Long before the decline, God led a group of planters to plant the church at its current location. Where she sits today is a testament to the faithfulness of past believers and God. The revitalization pastor must understand that the dire situation the church finds itself in did not happen overnight, thus it will not be restored overnight. The faithfulness of God has not left the property, and he is still working if his people will choose to work where he is overseeing.

Remember that if the growth happened decades ago, it could happen today. Still, it takes a determination to evaluate the effectiveness of every program and position within the church and have a willing spirit to adapt to the needs of today's community. Coming to terms with the current circumstances takes a holy boldness that a revitalizer can bring forth, an act of courage to challenge traditions and to establish God's reality for today in the local church. This step can be painful but also promising if the remnant

---

1. Bickford, "Thinking of a Replanter."

Prologue

is willing to surrender their will to God's will. The terms of engagement for today may look vastly different from yesterday, but if God is in it, he will restore this work for his glory.

Serving in a hard place can cause a pastor only to see the negative and miss the God moments weekly. A revitalization pastor needs to remember that the most significant breakthroughs come from the most incredible battles. Celebrating the successes from the week before, however small, is a crucial component to a turnaround. In years past, a candle would be lit near the pulpit as a reminder to the people that someone had won a soul the week before. While the candle did not save the soul, the visual effect was a powerful reminder that God was still at work. When someone is helped through the church—a soul won, a gift given, a prayer presented—it is a reminder that God has acted through his church to help someone in need. While it may seem insignificant to do simple acts of service, it is essential to God and should be celebrated.

Let me encourage you to celebrate the small wins, which I promise will add up to larger and larger wins for the church over time. Momentum begets momentum, and in a revitalization effort, every little bit helps restore a sense of success inside the church's walls. Allow personal professions of celebration to take place during each service, celebrate with weekly social media posts, and allow the spirit of celebration to light the darkness and overtake the heaviness of the past with the present reality of spiritual success. Know this truth: how a revitalization pastor acts in the ups and downs is vital to the health of the local church and is important to God. Too many pastors miss their destiny because they leave a revitalization effort too soon, burned out from the work, frustrated by progress or lack thereof, and longing for something new. Feeling this way is natural when serving in the hard places of ministry, but do not make the mistake of leaving too early before God has used you according to his plan. Commit to continuing to press forward in obedience, surrender to his will, and follow the path that has been laid out before you. Your time and that of the church is coming.

Addition through Subtraction

As a revitalizer embraces the call to the work that needs to be done, one must remember that the calling will not be completed in twelve or twenty-four months; most realistically, it will take years to begin to see a turnaround. Far too many pastor/church relationships break down before the effectiveness of the revitalization measures can be evaluated. Commit to continuing to move forward even when you feel like no one is following. Commit today to staying the course even when the work seems not to be going anywhere. Remember that God does the most extraordinary work in the hard places and reveals his love for the church. The downturn in the church took decades to accomplish, and the revitalization efforts may last much longer, but with a willing spirit, God can turn the tide of decline.

Serving in the hard places is all about finding ways to care, come, celebrate, and commit to the church to which God has called the revitalizer. God still shows up in the hard places where pastors toil away, seemingly alone, ignored by colleagues, and forgotten by the community. God calls new life to spring forth in these death chambers, but it takes a tenacious revitalizer to hold fast amid the negative headwinds that seem to mast around the local church. Through a tacit understanding of what has to occur, a commitment to prayer, and a heart willing to do the hard work, God will restore the local church.

Dr. Desmond Barrett

1

Staying Focused when Difficulty Comes

As I turned into the church's parking lot, my mind was a blur as I raced through all the scenarios and felt the uncertainties related to possibly becoming the pastor of this potential church. As I turned off the car, my eyes darted around the property, pausing every few seconds as if I was taking pictures for a future review in my mind in the weeks to come. My children's voices woke me from this trance and brought me back to the reality that I would be the candidate on display in just a few minutes as the church and her leadership would evaluate my worthiness to become their next pastor.

As the car door opened, I took a deep breath, taking in the scene of the property. The well-established traditional brick church had a giant white steeple that reached heaven, or so it seemed. The green grass of the parsonage yard was offset by the white picket fence that shaped its edges, and two maturing trees shaded a portion of the yard. In the distance, a large field held a playground and picnic shelter, beckoning families like mine to come to play. The night before, I missed most of this scene, as the nerves had clouded my view. The church board seemed warm but unsure about the church's future or the candidate they had before them. It would be

Addition through Subtraction

a frank interview where the church leadership would ask probing questions and I would provide rather blunt answers, as I was still uncertain of the calling to this new assignment. In a way, I was seeking a sign from God that this was the new community of faith where he was calling me.

Roused from the voices inside my vehicle, I exited the car with my family. Greeted by a board member, I instantly engaged in small talk about this or that, but nothing materially important. My son, ever eager to keep moving forward, waved to my wife and daughter to move on from this conversation. It was in this opening of space that the board member put on a big smile and reached for my hand, and as we shook hands, he slipped two crisp $100 bills into my palms. Wow! What a blessing to see the outpouring of love from what ostensibly was a stranger. That would be my high point with this board member and his wife. For the next three years, our relationship would be rocky, to say the least, and nonexistent for most of the time. Within months of coming to the church, he left leadership, withheld tithes, and left the church altogether. After a few months, the couple came back, warm and inviting, but sadly, a pattern began to develop where they would get silently mad about something and disappear for months on end, only for me to visit and encourage them, and they would come back.

In the final months of my pastorate, the church was moving toward a building campaign. This couple saw it as a waste of resources. Along with two other couples, they began to aggressively try to convince individuals and spouses to vote against the project. Each Sunday as I would finish my sermon, you would see them fan out across that small sanctuary, pull a different couple aside, and begin the arm twisting to end the project before it began. Ultimately, their view won out, and feeling disheartened, I left the church, leaving them to continue to maneuver God's church in a way that I knew was harmful—but like many pastors before, I did nothing to stop them out of fear of losing members. I wish I could say that things changed after I left, but sadly, the same pattern repeated itself, and they left the church again.

Staying Focused when Difficulty Comes

A Crucial Member Who Becomes Critical

What do you do when you lose a crucial member of the church? If you have served in church leadership for any amount of time, you have probably felt this loss. It seems personal if you are on the receiving end of why the person left. As a pastor or church leader, you need to honestly assess what happened and how the pattern could be stopped in the future. In reviewing the postmortem of this fallen relationship, the leadership must ponder the question of whether it is healthy for the church to subtract a negative member before adding a new member. Allow the thoughts and resources from the pages to follow to marinate in your soul before answering the question.

Ministry is challenging in a traditional year, but ministering during a pandemic has brought new challenges that seemed unheard of two years ago. With a new variant of COVID-19 taking hold as I sit down to write, members not returning, and the mandate for change fought at every turn, church leadership is facing a crisis like never before. Many churches have seen the loss of 40 to 50 percent of their average weekly attendance early on and the numbers are settling around a 25 percent non-return rate.[1] Others are seeing members return sparingly since the reopening. For the established church, this double whammy of the new variant of COVID-19 and legacy issues has created a critical mass where the critical spirit of members has taken hold.

When a key leader (staff member, teacher, board member, or large tither) leaves the church, the pastor's first reaction is to do anything and everything to keep them, even if it is a detriment to the ministry and church health. I have thought many times about what would have happened if I had let the couple go in my previous church and not kept wooing them to come back. What opportunity was lost by trying to love them back into the community of faith? Maybe as you read those words, you began to think, "You were Jesus." Still others might say, "You should have let them go."

---

1. Information gathered from traveling around six districts of my denomination and speaking with pastors and district leaders.

The truth is that these seemingly small decisions made daily impact a ministry for the long term. I have come to view these small decisions as windows of time that lay the foundation for success or failure in the established church. It all begins with the pastor seemingly making an insignificant decision that has a lasting impact.

Addition through Subtraction

What if the crucial member were not as vital as you first thought? What if the crucial member were a critical member that was holding back the church? Think about it this way: what if the person's subtraction (leaving the church) became an addition for the body? Okay, did I lose you there? If you are confused, do not give up on this resource just yet. Stay with me as I unpack what I have learned leading established churches. Be honest with yourself—leadership can be challenging through any loss, but when someone leaves on purpose and in turn blames you, it's gut-wrenching. Know this truth: God has a plan for the local church, and if you are willing to surrender to God's plan, great things will come from the loss. God revealed to me several years ago ways to look at subtraction as addition and to see it as a positive and not a negative.

For every season in the church's life, God brings forth the right person at the right time. However, for many churches, the person is so synonymous with the position that they become one and the same. When the crucial leader chooses to leave, it seems to onlookers that the position/program will fall apart. This is when the established church pastor has an opportunity to to reject this outlook by celebrating the person more than the position.

Throughout Scripture, God has raised leaders up from the remnants of those left behind to lead the church. So why not in the church today? Instead of fretting over a loss, focus on the person who is leaving the position. When my worship leader left abruptly, I was sad that I could not personally celebrate him, but the church made a point to thank him publicly for his service during the next worship service. Even if a person leaves a position in a way that does not honor the church, thank them for serving. Use it as an opportunity to share that God is already calling a new leader and that God has a plan for the established church.

When an opening occurs in the church, the first thing you probably want to do is fill the void. But let me encourage you to slow down and pray. Rushing in and filling the position with a warm body without praying, seeking wise counsel from others, and waiting on God can cause more pain in the long term. Leadership is not for everyone; trust that God has the right person for the season the church is in if the leader is willing to wait. Carefully selecting the next person is as important as having the next person in the position. Strategically, the pastor and leadership team must evaluate the critical components needed for the situation, the program's weaknesses, and who is best suited to bring their strengths to bear. See the opening as an opportunity to build a stronger team for the future and not simply as a gap in the leadership platform.

Think about it this way: Some people sit in the church who want to serve but do not know how or where. For some, they are wondering if they are welcomed to help. If asked, they would serve, but sadly, far too many are not invited. Use the loss of a crucial leader to create opportunities for people to help. If you have a greeting team that usually has four people, why not make it six or even rotate them? If you typically have two teachers per classroom for children, why not add a third? By creating opportunities and rethinking the leadership approach, the pastor makes room for a guest to move from guest to member and then to helper by connecting them within the church.

When you create opportunities for people to serve, people naturally step up and serve. When my worship leader left, three people stepped up to help lead singing and play instruments. That was God preparing for the new season. When my children's director stepped down after a great season of service, another dynamic duo stepped in and reshaped the program. That was God moving in ways I did not see coming. Time and time again, I have seen people want to help, but they must know where to help. Instead of falling apart when a crucial leader leaves, stand in faith; God has a plan and create spaces for guests to invest in.

Addition through Subtraction

Even if the proverbial sky is falling by all the losses, be an encourager rather than taking an unfavorable view. Often, the church turns to the opposing view when subtraction happens and begins to moan all the losses instead of seeing the losses as opportunities for addition—for God to do something new. Be a leader who projects confidence in the face of adversity. No one wants to follow a downcast leader, but they will follow a leader who projects a future-forward momentum that shares the concern of the loss but is committed to rebuilding the church one position at a time. Each position in the church is more significant than the person who holds the position. Leaders should always be forward-looking, forward focused, and forward driven as they move on from a loss.

Problematic Ministry Seasons

According to Peter Drucker, the founder of modern management, one of the most challenging jobs in America is to serve as a pastor.[2] While Drucker passed away in 2005, his thoughts rehashed here decades later speak to the heart of what pastors are facing daily. If the challenges of the established church are not met in Christ, the challenges will slowly bury a pastor's compassion and vision for the calling on their life. What calls the pastor to keep moving forward when the pastor wants to give up in a problematic ministry season? When a troublesome ministry period comes—and they will come—staying focused is essential to understanding the Master's plan.

In a season of discomfort, pastors find themselves looking down the road at growing ministries and begin to think, "Maybe I should change to fit what they are doing, because it seems to work." The mentality of greener pastures has caused division and envy in the church, forcing the church to miss opportunities to allow God to work through its leaders. Pastors are not superhuman, even when they think they are, as they face fears much like everyone else. The giftings that God has given the pastor are the right

---

2. O'Dell, "Toughest Job in America?," para. 1.

giftings for the church that he called the pastor to if the church enables the giftings to be used. A revitalizer must feel comfortable in the giftings or miss what God has for the pastor's ministry.

What sustains a pastor over the long haul is not the prestige, income, or pats on the back; it is the calling from God. Far too many pastors lose their way in ministry because they take their eyes off their calling and turn it to the worldly things around them. I get it—leaders want to be highly favored, but far too many serve in churches where they feel they are failing. While numbers are an essential indicator of a certain level of health within the church, numbers are not the be-all and end-all. A revitalizer's worth should not be found in numbers but in the lives impacted through the calling that they have answered. Sometimes, effectiveness is seen through growth in attendance, but the one-on-one discipleship opportunities are often missed, and only God knows their value. Pastors need to remember that their calling is not to the world but in God.

For the established church, many pastors serve bi-vocationally in the church. In reality, far too many pastors are full-time but getting bi-vocational pay, serving as the janitor, lawn-care worker, kitchen helper, etc. and working a full-time job in the community. What will it take for you or any pastor to ask for help? Sadly, too many of my colleagues have walked away from ministry frustrated and discouraged, because they did not build a team of servants around them to help support the church's work. Pastors cannot be at their very best if they are tired and frustrated and serve in areas where laypeople perform more effectively. Building a team of servants who are willing to teach is necessary. Over time, the pastor can hand off more significant tasks to those invested in the church through intentional discipleship, but first, discipleship must take place.

I have been there. The exhaustion of life weighs you down and you want to give up; it is there that I have found God. When things are going well in the pastor's home and ministry life, it is also there that God is found. God is in all things. As a leader, the pastor cannot allow anyone to put negative thoughts in their mind to distract them from their calling. See the good in all situations by finding simple pleasures in daily routines and peace when things do not go your way. Revitalizers who serve with longevity have found simple pleasures to sustain them as they move forward on the most challenging days. Seeing good does not mean you overlook the bad, but it does mean you find God in all places and in all ways.

Pastoring today is not easy, as you could probably attest. Many mainline denominations do not have enough pastors to fill pulpits today—much less when baby boomers retire, as more will do within the next fifteen years. The stress on pastors will become more of a burden, but even with these headwinds, pastors will be able to find peace in the Savior by living in their giftings, following the calling, building a team around them, and seeing the good in everyday life.

Finding Hope when Hopeless

The first quarter of 2020 came in like a thief in the night and stole what many Christians saw as the church—its physical campus and corporate worship time. For many pastors, the spirit of fear crept in due to a lack of resources. Instead of seeing the negative, I believe God is helping pastors and churches to connect with people and his church in new ways. Whatever the church faces, see the crises as addition through subtraction—an opportunity to stand in Christ and not dwell in the crises.

Serving the church has changed since the pandemic. The pandemic has created an opportunity to expand ministry outside the four walls of the church. See the crises or unfavorable season the church is in as an opportunity to expand the ministry. Become the church to those in need. Enjoy the new chance to learn from other leaders and churches in how they connect to their community of believers and use best practices in your local context from what you have found.

Throughout the church's history, she has been challenged by forces of darkness and evil and has always overcome them. Even in the worst oppression, there was a mighty remnant of godly leaders who remained, who, in turn, were used by God to expand his kingdom. I believe deep in my soul today that God is challenging you as a leader in your local context to expand the kingdom by using technology and resources to spread the gospel in new and creative ways. I challenge you to search the Scriptures with your people and allow the words of the past to strengthen your present realities as you trust the process.

Do me a favor by pausing and thinking about this for a moment: How are you connecting with your people each week on and off campus? Are you using creative ways to communicate through Zoom, Facebook Live, Instagram pictures of encouragement, postcards, or telephone and text calls? When a critical spirit descends upon the church, your people need to know you care. You might not stop the pain, but you can connect relationally with the tools created for this time and share your love for the church with them. When you reach them, do not focus on the negative; focus on the positive and share the hope and love of Jesus Christ with them.

Finding hope in a hopeless situation is about giving your leadership back to God and knowing he will direct you amid the storm. Be an encouraged leader today. You can and will make a difference in your local church and the broader community if you use the problematic ministry season to learn from others. Lean into Scripture, love the people you have like never before, and do not stress the subtraction, because addition is heading your way.

2

Finding God's Promises in a Season of Change

I COULD HEAR IN my colleague's voice that he was worried. He had just sat through a rough board meeting where half of the board resigned over his handling of COVID-19. I listened as he walked me through the political and social divide that had overtaken his church. His typically confident and robust voice betrayed the hurt and sorrow he felt as he sat in his fresh wound. I struggled to find the right words to share with him as his pain poured out, and I felt powerless to help. As the conversation was nearing its natural end—or so I thought—he blurted out, "I should just quit!" At that moment, I realized that he was willing to subtract himself from the equation to help the church move forward toward addition. How many pastors have sacrificed their calling for the local church? How many have given up because members had given up on them? Each day, thousands of pastors contemplate quitting their assignment, and far too many do walk away from ministry altogether. Behind the Sunday smile lies pain that comes from the selfless sacrifices that the pastor has endured. Often, the role of pastor comes with little praise and negative words that seem harsh and cutting from the people the pastor leads. Far too many pastors have lost the joy once found in ministry, revealing the pain left behind.

As I hung up the phone, I sat in silence, trying to redeem the space that had been taken over in my brain by negative thoughts and emotions. My colleague was brokenhearted, and sadness reverberated throughout my body for him. In that dark moment, isolated in my thoughts, the Son of God reminded me that only he could direct the local church. Only under his authority and power could the established church be saved in a moment of crisis, and only he could help my friend.

A Changing Church

The church you had before COVID-19 is not the same church that you will have in the future. A cultural shift has taken place outside the church walls and has now reverberated within her borders. Churches with personality or program-driven church settings must face the reality that personalities and programs will not be enough to attract people to attend the church weekly. With many in the community limiting contact outside of their families, this has dramatically changed how the church operates. The relic of opening the doors of the church and then the people coming has died with yesteryear. Online services and small-group engagements will become more critical in the future. The development of micro churches, where there are small gatherings of believers spread out over a geographic area, will become the norm. The main campus will become a meeting place for other ministries and nonprofits and will act as a host of community services. The church will be transitioning from a once-a-week meeting place to a compassionate ministry center where people are in the building throughout the week receiving help through a host of programs. As the church begins to shift to adapt to the new reality of a post-pandemic church, subtraction will become the norm early on, as people will resist change.

Leader, surrender today your idea of what the church should look like and focus on the kingdom mandate that comes in a

Addition through Subtraction

season of change. Realize now that you will not be able to stop or even slow down the subtraction that will come with a shift in focus as the church seeks to become a neighbor to the community through community outreach. When you serve in faith, Christ will bring forth the addition if you trust the process.

As change enters the church's foyer, there will be those who resist the transition from inside and others who will leave in protest. Learn that you cannot control how members act or react to the changes in society, but you do have control in how you respond and how you feel. For far too long, members had their idea of what the church should look like, and for many, it was a non-biblical view. COVID-19 has forced members and, ostensibly, the church to grapple with the new reality that the church has changed for good. Face coverings, sanitization stations, limited gatherings, political fault lines, and culture wars have overtaken the norm and become the new norm within the church's walls.

Revitalizers will have to trust God as they lead through these new minefields of disenchantment. Instead of being discouraged by members leaving, pastors should focus on what they can control. The pastor can preach biblically based sermons that draw attendees to repentance, prayer, and service while focusing on the new vision for the church. Pastors should lead by example—through small-group gatherings that focus on others rather than always on the church's needs—by pointing people to the Savior through serving in a Christlike way.

Realize that it is not by accident that you are pastoring in a time of eminent change in the global church. God has divinely appointed the one in charge of the local church to be the pastor and to lead with passion and commitment. In a season of change, the pastor has an opportunity to preach, teach, and serve with conviction, knowing that God has called the one to help in the local church for such a time as this, and it is a gift to remember the calling God has placed on the pastor's life. As COVID-19 has challenged the cultural norms like never before, be encouraged to know that the cutting edge of a new awakening is upon the church. The awakening is spiritual and physical, as the church is shifting from being a Sunday-morning-only church to a church that serves daily in the community.

Seeing God in the Change

As the church adapts to the new reality that change has come, the established church pastor will sense the pushback from those holding firmly to tradition. The pushback is not against the pastor but against the change that has come forth. Members will hold tightly to something that should have been God's, because they have an ownership stake in it. The pastor's role should be to support struggling members but permit them to leave if they keep threatening, because obedience to God is more important than obeying man. Remember, control does not rest in a single member or a small group of resistant fighters but with God and the vision he has given. God reminded me in my spirit as I prayed during a season of change that it would be alright if I let people go. I pestered God for a little more revelation that it would work out. He provided me with methods of reacting to change that encouraged my soul and calmed my nerves.

God knows I like to have order in my life and ministry. During a recent season of change, the sense of order in my life hung in the balance. With each disagreement and family leaving the church, it challenged my control focus. While it was painful, it was an essential part of the revitalization process to see God amid the change. One night as I lay in bed praying, God reminded me that he is in control and that I needed to trust him. I thought, "I am a pastor, and I do trust you, Lord." Yet, I wasn't trusting him with everything. Being so focused on numbers—who I had gained, who I had lost, the next project, what needed tweaking, getting people back into service, and collecting the offering to pay bills—I was not accepting that he was in control. It came to me clearly: stop trying to do everything when you do not control anything. What I needed to do was focus on what I could manage. I could manage my prayer life, devotional time, and alone time with God. Everything else I could guide but not control—only God could.

Addition through Subtraction

Change is not easy. Let me say that again, just in case you skipped over that sentence. Change is not easy. Did you highlight that sentence? Because when it gets hard and you want to give up, I want you to go back to that sentence. In the church world, it seems that change can scare many out of following Jesus. The world around the members is changing quickly and then adding new people and programs; it is no wonder people want to subtract themselves from the process. What used to be right is now considered wrong in the world's eyes, and the one thing that church members could count on in the past was the church not changing—until now. As a leader, you need to realize that change is necessary if the message of hope is to reach the population's needs today. While the message never changes, methods do. The church must be flexible in adapting to the change that is needed. Do yourself a favor: do not stress yourself when evaluating the needs of the church. If a program or space is no longer working for the needs of your church post-COVID-19, then shift and adapt to the new condition. For many churches, worship spaces are too large. With 25 percent of the church not returning post-COVID-19, reducing seating is an option to create a unique atmosphere to worship in, changing a classroom into a pantry to feed the community, and using other unused space for families who need internet access for online schooling. Adapting to community changes can force the church to adapt to meet the need.

When change occurs, many will celebrate the accomplishment, but a small few will try to impede the progress to hold fast to traditions that they are used to experiencing in the church. As a leader, be willing to celebrate the past but progress forward without regard to your legacy. Looking out for their legacy can trap a leader into doing only the safe things and not the "God things" in the church. Throughout Scripture, God challenged and equipped grace-filled leaders who, in return, obeyed and did mighty things for the kingdom. In my spirit, I hear God saying the time is now for leaders like you to not worry about what others might say and press forward to what God is saying. Change is coming, one way or another, to the church. Doing nothing is a change in itself, because it means turning from a forward position to a retreat position, hoping that change will pass by the address where the church sits. Let me encourage you to be a leader who worries less about what other people think about your leadership ability and focuses more on obeying God's calling on your ministry.

As a revitalization leader, you cannot control how other people will feel or react to what is happening around the church as she begins to seek revitalization. You can, however, control how you respond to whatever situation you are facing. Make sure you speak, pray, and project a compassionate view of how God uses troubling times. Allow God to help create in you and in the church the ability to build a spiritual and physical life that honors him by coming back from the brink of closure to being a healthy, vibrant church.

One of the ways you can help the church is through leading through positive prayers, turning negative voices into positive ones. Realize that God is still on the throne; changes in the church are not a surprise to him. Lead your people in a positive worship experience where the Holy Spirit is welcomed into the service and the service is given to the glory of God. As a leader, your reaction to the situations coming against the church are watched by all, and leading with a positive and forward-leaning view can encourage others.

Remember, leader, that the church is not going to go back to the way it has always been run. God is an agent of change. Throughout the centuries, God has used people and situations just like you and your church to transform the church to meet the needs of that day. Today, he is working again. Trust him, celebrate him, and know God is working on behalf of the church.

A Promise Found in Change

Have you felt the pain of an extended season of loss due to members leaving? Reduced attendance, offerings, and gathering opportunities can leave an emptiness for those who still attend. You might feel burdened with trying to figure out the right course to chart in uncertain times. Some leaders have suggested closing the doors for good and finding another profession for themselves. I do not think

Addition through Subtraction

that is God's plan for you or the local church. God reminds us that he is the Rock, and if we build his church on his word, we will make it if the church seeks the promise found in change.

How many times have you heard, "I wish things would return to normal"? It is becoming more apparent that things will not return to "normal" for some time, and maybe that is a good thing. For too long, the church has operated the same way week after week, with slight deviation or room for the Holy Spirit to move. The church is broken, and God is calling her back to centering herself again on him. A time of intentional prayer focusing on what God wants for the church and what he wants for his people is coming. See it as an opportunity not to be lost in past programs or even past decisions and to hear God's voice afresh for the church's season ahead. Leading your people in intentional, dedicated prayer times will recenter the church back on Christ and prepare the way for the future. Find a night and develop a small group where prayer warriors gather to cry out to God. Prayer matters. Prayer works. Get praying!

As you pray, permit yourself to go smaller to grow back healthier. Revitalization is all about dying to self and rising in the Savior. It is about learning that it is okay to subtract to add. While it goes against everything you might feel or even want, subtraction is needed if God is to get the glory in a revitalization effort. Maybe your church is running less than it did before the pandemic. Begin to imagine God in the less, and you will realize you have more. More faith. More compassion. More Jesus. What an opportunity to become an Acts-driven church, where the church is not about numbers but about meeting together in small groups to share life. Small groups do not have to be an afterthought in expanding ministry but at the forefront of returning the local church to its biblical mandate and roots. Jesus showed that smaller is better when developing a team of ministry leaders to reach people with the gospel effectively. With twelve men, he helped change the world. With three men, he prayed. Now, imagine—with the number of people in your church—what would happen if they grew smaller to go deeper to come back larger? What a radical transformation would take place in them, in the group, and in the larger church. The church knows its members have become scattered. Some have disconnected from being a part of the church. Programs that once attracted members to attend are seen today as a threat to their health if they gather in large masses. The fear of catching COVID-19 or of changing the way things have always been done has lured the once-faithful people to stay away or storm away.

In this new period, programs are not what people want; they want to feel connected. For months, many were isolated away from family, friends, and routines. Many left the church, because the focus was on anything other than God. The church has an opportunity to fill the void by reconnecting with the disconnected. Telephone calls, text messages, social media touchpoints, meals out with guests, and old-fashioned snail mail can make people feel that they are part of something greater than themselves. Christ taught the early church to connect to the people on the margins. Connecting with people to share Christ's love, encouragement, and hope for the future is a formula to build a robust and healthy church.

The one key point that many revitalizers miss is that you have to lead with adaptability in mind. They rush in and rush to get things done instead of adapting their desires to God's desires and the needs of people in the the local context. By now, you realize that you cannot control what is happening to you, but you can control how you react to the prescribed changes around you. The rapid amount of change should be an opportunity to evaluate everything, not change everything in the first six months. Evaluate the essentials of worship and what is being elevated above worship, and discard the latter. Worship is not just music but can become an idol in the church that keeps people from glorifying God. From nameplates to named rooms, icons have taken hold of the church. Being adaptable is taking away sacred cows and replacing them with God-focused ministry and items that enhance the worshiper's understanding of their faith by allowing them to grow deeper with God. For too many churches, things have become idols and have taken away the valid reason people come to church. Use this time to change the old ways of hosting church. Do not be constrained by

Addition through Subtraction

the past but adapt to the present situation and needs of the church, and do it with God's promotion, not worldly desires, at the center.

Finding God in a season of change is about surrendering your will to God's will in your life and ministry. Be encouraged—God is still on the throne, and he will work this out for the church's good if the church is willing to do its part in building the kingdom.

3

Reestablishing the Spiritual Center

CHANGE HAPPENS WHEN THE leader least expects it. Leadership is about adapting to change quickly by reestablishing the spiritual center to encourage others to move from crisis to Christ. In my work as a revitalizer and as an executive director of a soup kitchen and food pantry, I share with people regularly that God has given his people five Ps to help reestablish a leader's spiritual center after facing change.

Process What Has Happened

Change creates an opportunity to discern the will of God for a revitalizer's ministry. Change in any form has a way of clearing through the unimportant things to expose what is essential in a leader's life and thought processes. For change to be effective, the leader must process what has happened, then pivot by evaluating how it happened, why it happened, and what can be learned from the process. Processing the change enables the leader to establish benchmarks of understanding that will allow the church to move forward past the subtraction season and into the next phase of addition.

It is not easy to lead a person who does not respect your leadership style. As I stood at the very top of a stairwell leading to the teen room, my church-board secretary came storming up the steps. I could tell by the look on her face that she was unhappy, and for the life of me, I could not figure out why. Within seconds, she let me know where I had failed her, the church, and the community outreach initiative she had put together. She cursed me in word and spirit, which left me shell-shocked in the aftermath. I stumbled into a chair after the volley of threats, demands, and accusations, and just sat there numb from the experience I had just lived through. That night and in the coming days, I spent time processing the pain that I was experiencing and that I had inexplicably caused my board secretary. I realized that I could not change what had happened, but I could learn from it and become a better leader.

Pivot with a Purpose

If the process is about evaluating the change, the objective (reestablishing the spiritual center) is about pivoting away from the change. Leaders who grow through a season of change take away nuggets of knowledge and apply them to the latest phase of their ministry. Pivoting comes from understanding the purpose of what has happened and then learning all that you can from the difficult season. The revitalizer should seek out truths and then lean into what has been discovered to gain the most from the pivotal moment.

I realized I could not control the circumstances or even the outcome of the conversation with my board secretary, but I could control my reaction to it. The following day after the incident, I made it a point to visit with her, apologize for anything she felt I did wrong, and seek her forgiveness. As I shared these sentiments, she began to cry and apologize to me for how she had acted. She shared that she had been under a lot of stress, and I was the conduit for her pain.

If I had never submitted myself to a board member, I would have missed ministering to her through her pain to see God's restoration of the relationship. Pivoting with a purpose is all about honoring God's calling on your ministry and obeying the Holy Spirit.

Prepare for the Future

As the pastor reestablishes the spiritual center in their leadership, they can prepare for God's future for the ministry. This preparation season is a short window of opportunity to advance the kingdom ministry forward. There is a tendency for those who have gone through a crisis to rest. During this stage of reestablishment, God wants to advance the future forward instead of pausing many times. I read some time ago a sign that said, "The future is now!" "Now" means not waiting but advancing up the spiritual field to gain ground for future ministries that God has planned. Preparation is not about waiting but wanting what God wants in his timing.

Prioritize the Needs in Front of You

Reestablishing their spiritual center allows the leader to embrace God's vision for the ministry. Have you known a leader who was so driven that they drove in the wrong direction and lost their way in Christ? Or have you been such a leader? Prioritizing what is important to God, God's people, and then themself will enable the leader to be a follower of Christ and not a driver of Christ. There are many former Christians who felt pushed rather than lead into the presence of the Lord, and God uses a crisis in the church to make clear what his priorities are supposed to be. Do not get trapped in what has been and miss what God is saying should be. Prioritize the needs that God has called you to focus on as you recenter your and your church's spiritual lives.

Propel Forward God's Dreams

Realize that what has been lost in a crisis can be regained in Christ. God is a forward-moving God. He is never stagnant or backward leaning. God is a God of second, third, and fourth chances, because he wants you to progress. What are the dreams that he has for you? What is the vision he has for your ministry? Do not allow a challenging situation or season define who you are as a leader. Instead, enable it to propel you forward into the dreams God has planned for you. Know this nugget of truth: the best days of your ministry are not behind you. The good ole days are not as good as the days yet undiscovered. Unwrap what God has for you, your church, and the lives that will be impacted through your ministry. Dream dreams again and become the leader God has called you to be.

I wish I could write that my relationship with the church-board secretary got better. It did for a short time, but she and I would bump heads time and time again. In the final months of my ministry at that church, she sat out of the service and waited until I left the church to return. I have wondered what would have happened if she and I were able to work together as a team. She was so talented in many ways, but sadly, our personalities or the lack of a deep, meaningful relationship hindered us from coming together.

Unpacking the God Potential inside Your Church

What is your church doing to prepare for the next season of ministry? Churches fighting to rebound from decline begin to declutter the clutter that has held the established church back. Revitalized churches used the downtime related to the pandemic to attain God's promise for the church through evaluation, renovation, and motivation to move into the next season of life in the local church. It is not too late to lead your leadership team through a self-evaluation of the church and unpack the God potential.

With fewer people attending on a typical Sunday, the church needs have shifted from programmatic, cafeteria-style offerings to service programs intended to streamline programs when the church sees fewer workers but more community needs. By evaluating all aspects of the church's life, the leadership team can see what works and what has outlived its usefulness. Evaluating is not just a task to look inward but an opportunity to look outward toward the community by matching the giftings of the church members to the needs within the community. While this can be a painful process to the entrenched, longtime church member, it is necessary if the church is to grow under God's leadership and anointing. Change, while not easy, will become rewarding when the church submits to God's authority and realizes the plans God has for the local church.

When you think of the word "renovation," you may instantly think of knocking out walls, and maybe that is part of it. In unpacking a church's potential, renovating has more to do with the church's mind, body, and spirit to serve in the season they currently find themselves in than reconstruction of the church building. Think back to when pioneers planted your church. The planters saw a need and sought ways to meet that need through a church. Today, the culture, community context, and conditions have changed, but far too many churches have not moved on from the same programs, positions, and partnerships since they began. The renovation spirit is about reviewing all facility needs to meet current and future needs.

An example of this is that my church moved classrooms two years ago to accommodate a more extensive teen program. We are moving them again into a new wing to accommodate their needs and expand the children's ministry two years later. Adaptability is the central theme with a renovation mindset and, if done correctly, will be rewarded.

Losing people through subtraction connected to the church is painful for a long time but also necessary when God brings about a new thing in the church's life. A church must ask themselves: What motivates our church to stay the same? Comfortableness and routine make up the primary reason churches do not move outside their current circumstances. But is that God's plan for the local church? I think not. God has called the church to make Christlike disciples, which becomes the central motivation for church leaders who move the church to unpack its potential and move toward addition. Churches have to stop chasing after those who want to leave and motivate those who choose to stay. When someone rejects the church, I always say, "I am thankful for what they did during the season they were here." I realize that not everyone is supposed to be here forever. Permit yourself to say goodbye in

Addition through Subtraction

order to say hello to the new members and service opportunities that God has for the local church.

I know God wants to bless the local church, but the church has to get out of God's way to let it happen. Be a leader who evaluates, renovates, and motivates your local church to become the church God has called her to be.

The Plan for Renewal

By now, you realize that you are not alone. The struggles of the established church are real regardless of which denomination you serve. For the last decade plus, I have served as a pastor in the established church, and in my experience, God still wants to do a new work amid what can seem to be a crisis if we allow Christ to move.

A church that is going to renew itself for the future and move from decline to growth is a church that needs to have a prayer life that shows it trusts God with everything. Churches have to move from the show-and-tell model to the serve-and-go model of doing church. Hear my heart; I am not against developing a service that honors God and is attractive to those who do not attend your church, but that cannot be the primary focus. We have too many "nightclub" churches as it is. We need faith-filled, anointed prayer centers where the spirit of God is ushered in and where, in return, through prayer, the power of his work—not just man's work—is seen in a given service.

Where is prayer in the service? For many, including my own church, prayer has been regulated to two minutes in the middle of the service. Knowing that we do not adequately pray enough, I have added a dedicated time of prayer that is laypeople driven on Wednesday nights, plus prayer times privately throughout the week. If the church is going to see a decisive move of God, prayer must be foundationally built in a prayer closet. When the church trusts God for the increase, it begins to move from an inward-focused posture to an outward-looking stance that prioritizes others over self. It is at that moment that the church starts to turn from subtraction to a spirit of addition. The church's mission is found in the word of God, not in the mouths of humanity. The mission is to make Christlike disciples. So, if that is the church's mission, then everything she does has to be pointed in the direction of reaching the community with the gospel of Christ.

When a church enters a revitalization effort, many pastors move to update the mission statement of the church. Why change it? Why not capture the essence of the mission statement and connect it back to the biblical mission statement given by God? Unless it is non-biblical, keep the mission statement. Evaluate where the church can walk alongside a local or global ministry to expand the kingdom and move the mission field from inside the church to the streets. The goal of the missional church is not to duplicate services but to fill the void in the community through sowing generously of their time, talents, and treasure.

When the people's heart becomes the eyes to love those hurting, the church becomes the community of faith the neighborhood desires. By reaching outside instead of focusing within, the church begins to rebound from decline to vitality. Reestablishing the fundamental mission of God in the local context is about honoring and following God's plans. Sure, numbers matter, but do not let that control the church. Value as a church should not be placed in worship attendance alone. Value is seen in the people inside and outside of the church. When the church connects with the community, value is built and God is glorified.

As the established church faces decline, leadership must evaluate all aspects of the church (programs, positions, and power) by inspecting what is working, what is not working, and what needs to be added or subtracted. Throughout this process, the Bible should be the church's guide. The word of God needs to be elevated above all else. Churches that revitalize from decline are churches that read the word, hear the word preached, teach the word in small/large groups, and see the word lived out.

The fact that a church has plateaued or declined should not be seen as bad leadership but as an opportunity to redirect the church from self to Savior. Then, it moves from Savior to others over time. The people who make up the local church must self-evaluate by

Addition through Subtraction

reflecting on whose church it is. Once the members realize that it is God's church and God's design, the church can begin to reflect on four areas of service:

- Serve with excellence in every way. Everything should be done to God's glory.
- Serve with passion for finding, reaching, and winning the lost.
- Serve with a commitment to being in the King's service until he calls the church home, and never give up when the field becomes hard to plow.
- Serve for those who live in the community, not just church members.

While practical, the steps shared above are realistic to accomplish through selfless evaluation. Reestablishing the spiritual center starts with you, the leader. If you want your church to change, you have to change. Are you willing? If so, then begin the hard work inside, then start to work with your congregation. Lead your church congregation one person at a time. See the result in pieces and begin to put the pieces together to share the larger picture of Christ to the church. Revitalizing the established church is all about becoming a fully committed church serving God over self, which takes work. It starts with personal prayer times, corporate prayer, and community-centered prayer where the congregation prayers for community needs.

If you are ready, God can help. Ready, set, grow!

4

For God's Glory

THE CHURCH SEEMS EMPTY. The parking lot only has a couple of cars in her large lot. There appears to be no life left in the once-thriving church. In a last-ditch effort to save the church, the church board hires a pastor with a family, believing that a younger pastor will save the church. When the pastor begins to change the "way it has always been done," there is strong pushback. Over time, the pastor's efforts to revitalize the church are thwarted at every turn. Out of frustration more than a calling, the pastor leaves the church to become the pastor of another church. Sadly, this scenario plays out weekly in dying churches all over America. How can this stop? Churches must begin asking themselves: Is this God's best for the church—to die in self-rule over God's rule? If a church is to move from the death spiral into stabilization and, eventually, healthy growth, the church has to realize that the church is not "ours" but "His."

Far too many churches are tucked away off busy streets, an island unto themselves—a club—more than a religious center, with the full benefits of membership and fellowship but isolated from the calling to serve the community. If one were to dig into the church's history, they would find that it wasn't one singular decision that was made to isolate themselves from the neighborhood but slow, steady

Addition through Subtraction

subtractions that drew the walls closer and closer in on themselves. While subtraction was sometimes decades in the making, addition will not come in the form of a turnaround with one blockbuster outreach event or even several throughout the year. Instead, it will come through a consistent outward focus where members walk in partnership with the needs of the community.

If the church wants to move from lip service to community service, it must serve the community with a God-centered focus rather than an us-centered focus. I will be honest—this takes lots of prayers, a fully surrendered spirit, and deliberant outreach where the focus is on the agency, program, or person in the community rather than the church. Stop and ask yourself: Who is running the church? God? The pastor? Or the church boss(es)? The temptation in a declining church is for a member or members to cling tightly to control, because they are invested in seeing the church stay open. Too often, the investment that was started out of a place of love for the church is quickly overtaken by pride and arrogance that they are the only ones who can save the church. This misplaced authority eliminates the authority of God and Scripture and hardens their unwillingness to cede control over to the pastor or new attendees in the church. Fiefdoms become the norm, and the kingdom of God becomes less and less. While outsiders may realize that this is scripturally backward and threatens the spirit of God within the church, the church boss tightens their grip on the church, fast-forwarding decline.

Biblically, lay leaders are not the called leaders of the local church. God has called an under-shepherd to lead the local flock in the mission and vision that he has spelled out for every church, including yours. If a church is to grow spiritually healthy, they have to resubmit to the authority of Scripture and God's called pastor and allow God to lead them forward. As the church lies slowly dying, the memories of days long past seem to engulf the church. Tokens of celebration (memorial plaques, a room dedicated to a church member, etc.) become golden calves that enshrine the church in idol worship. What was meant for good has become the final nails drilled into the coffin of the soon-departing church.

Revitalization is not about death but about celebrating the past, evaluating the present, and preparing for the future. It is about restoring what has been lost (families, neighborhood relevancy, and Christlike community) by letting go of past practices to claim what God has for the church today. It does not mean a church has to forget its history, but it does mean they cannot cling to that history, or the church will become history.

Throughout Scripture, God did a new thing using an ancient thing (his word, his guidance, and people's obedience) to build his kingdom. Restoring the established church is about restoring the church's relationship with God over attachment to things. Submission is not easy in a dying church, but it is needed if the church will become the church that Christ has called her to be in this season of her life. If you and your people want to add, you have to subtract your desires so that you can have God's. Prayer is the central element of a turnaround. Prayer, which leads to repentance for past wrongs and hurts that the church has caused, is crucial in evaluating where members of the church have been and where God wants to take them. Restoration comes to a church when she can see past wrongs, seek forgiveness, repent, and turn from troubled ways. The church's legacy is not a negative one but one of grace when seen through the eyes of renewal and not stagnation. To win the community, the church must first win the spiritual war inside the church through prayer. Prayer cannot be a two-minute bullet point printed in the bulletin as part of the weekly service lineup but instead an intentional part of who the church is becoming. Repairing past hurts will not mask that those hurts affected people, but it will prepare hearts for what God wants to do within the church. Ultimately, prayer positions the power of God to prepare the way forward to make the church a community-centered church.

Let me give you a warning that I will repeat in several areas throughout the book: Change is not easy, or it would already come about. Change brings out the worst in people when the change arrives at their ministry doorstep. Change can cause church splits or, at the very least, significant fights within the church. Who wins when change is denied or delayed because of a powerful cluster of people in the church? The devil. The evil one wants nothing more than to sow division and discord within the walls of the church. If the demonic forces can keep God's people fighting inside, they will miss opportunities to expand the kingdom of God outside her walls. Churches that revitalize overtime adapt to the changing nature of their time and community needs. Sometimes, that means programmatic or wholesale structural change within the church.

Instead of protecting programs, the church turns from professing Christ with mere words to partnering with agencies and groups that reach people groups that the church is not currently reaching. A gospel-centered, Christ-focused church is a church that walks alongside people to make Christlike disciples. That takes intentionality and adaptability. I promise that if you take a step toward your neighbors, God will bring addition.

By now, you might have asked yourself: Can a church be saved after years in the death spiral? The simple answer is yes. If there is a remnant of believers who will allow themselves to be the spark of renewal, God can use them to light the match. Revitalization is about rekindling the passion for what God wants to do amid death. Scripture reminds the reader that old bones can come alive again (see Ezek 37:1–10) if there is willingness to move past problems through prayer and into a spirit of passion for the lost. Everything that the church has done in the past must be assessed for gospel effectiveness. If a program does not reach people for Christ, then the program should be retired to prepare for a program that will enable the church to reach the community in a new way. Ask yourself: How bad does the church want addition? How far are you willing to lead them?

As part of the refining process, turnaround leaders should pray for new people to lead or for current members to rekindle their passion for the lost so that the church can become an effective field hospital for the sick. Established church leader, the church of Jesus Christ is not dead. While a building may lay dormant and his people scattered, the church of Christ is very much alive. For far too long, the world has had a hold of the church and has slowly killed her. I believe in my soul that by you reading this book, you are taking the necessary steps to say to the church that it is time that we take back the power from the world by becoming a church built on the foundation of Christ as her Cornerstone.

Reconnecting to the Christ Story Happening inside the Church

Picture it in your mind: the pastor stands to enter the pulpit and looks up and realizes that hardly anyone is there. The once-active church is in a state of decline. The pastor has done his best to lead the church into renewal, but feels like giving up. Is that you? Is that your church? Pastors are hurting, discouraged, and ready to throw in the towel. I get it, but realize that 65 percent of churches in the United States have less than one hundred people regularly attending.[1] In my own tribe, the Church of the Nazarene in USA/Canada, 76.6 percent of churches are made up of less than one hundred people, and of those, 50 percent have less than fifty people attending weekly, according to 2020 statistics from the Nazarene Research Center.[2]

Yet, pastors get caught looking over the fence at the large, growing church down the road and wondering: Did God forget me? Did God forget my church? They don't realize their church is not small or even average—it is the traditional size of churches in North America.

When I view the church, I have hope in the God story that is taking shape within her four walls. An established church that is declining is not alone. Dr. Nina Gunter, general superintendent emeritus for the Church of the Nazarene, spoke at a conference and said, "The church is not in crisis; the church is in Christ."[3] That one sentence changed my ministry outlook regarding the local church, and I pray it does for you too. Maybe you need to pause and highlight and reflect on that sentence. Christ is still with you in your

---

1. Earls, "Small Churches," para. 5.
2. Laura K. Lance, email message to author, August 5, 2021.
3. Gunter, "Good News," para. 7.

church. He has called you. He cares for you and the people you shepherd weekly. You are not alone in this fight, as God is with you.

Everything done in the local church should be done to the glory of God. Begin to tell the God stories of how someone the church has prayed for had an answer to prayer. Tell the story of how a member blessed the community through a simple act of kindness. Tell the story of how God is leading his people to pray, seek, and help turn things around. If you have no story to tell, then go spend time investing in others and then share that story with your people. There is a story to tell, if you will tell it. Tell the story weekly in small groups and in corporate worship services. Celebrate weekly instead of procrastinating or overthinking about doing something as you help move the church forward in God's power. The story has been about subtraction long enough—now go talk about God's addition.

The story of revitalization is a story of redeeming what others have written off. Share with the church and others in the community how God is impacting lives and is still using your local church. Celebrate the renewal story in conversations, through social media, and in the pulpit. How many times have you gotten caught up in the negative and missed the positive? Instead of focusing on the negative, focus on the positive of what God is still doing.

I know it is easy to get caught in the negative cycle of not having enough money, not having enough people, etc., but get caught up in the fact that God has called you and each person who is connected and attends the church to pray for God's direction, prepare for God's move, and partake in God's plan. If you do your part and your people do their part, it will get better, and that is a God promise found in his word.

Revitalization is about falling forward and not falling backward. In a revitalization work, try something until it works. Do not give up! Keep trying even when it looks like no fruit is coming from it. Hear my heart: the church address is not by accident and your calling to the church to serve as the pastor is not by accident—this is a divine appointment to be an influencer in the local neighborhood, called by God. What an opportunity to live the story through communion with each other. Live the story in the community, through the calling that God has for the local church. Find organizations that need help and come alongside them and volunteer time. Find a school in the area that needs volunteers and support the school in their need. Find neighbors who need help and support them through yard work and other tasks. Christ has called the church to "go," not to stay in one place. Living the story means becoming the hands and feet of Christ in the neighborhood, and what a blessing to know the call and to obey it in serving your community.

Dethroning a Fiefdom in the Church to Recover God's Glory

I have dealt with many church members who have built their fiefdoms inside the local church throughout the years. Sometimes, it is a church boss or a well-meaning volunteer, but it is always a person who has taken their spiritual eyes off what is essential in the church's life—serving God by serving others. While fiefdoms are often associated with medieval times, they are seen more regularly in modern times in the local church. A fiefdom overseer oversees an area inside the church and claims ownership of the task or space as their territory. Left unchallenged, these gatekeepers create disputes, disruptions, distractions, and death inside the local church.

Fiefdoms in the church are not new. You can probably think of one or even several church members in your local church that has taken leadership to the extreme. These dedicated men and women have given their time and talents to help the church, but far too often they harm, not help, the church over time. What started as a ministry became a fiefdom for their wants and desires.

Over a seven-week period, I was challenged in my church as I tried rather unsuccessfully to navigate a fiefdom in the sound booth. What should have been an easy fix became a drawn-out process with deadlines missed and questions left unanswered that created tension and strife. In the corporate world, I would have fired the individual, but in the church, I extended grace.

Addition through Subtraction

It all started when a power surge hit the church, knocking out technical systems which were password protected. The volunteer in the sound booth controlled all these passwords and procedures and would not turn them over to me or anyone else that asked. The church member and I had always had an amicable relationship. So, I was shocked when he delayed, denied, and ignored my pleas to hand them over so the church could get a company to come in and fix the issues. This led me to remove him from his volunteer post, and he, in return, threatened to leave the church and call the district superintendent. What I really wanted to say was "Please call and leave shortly after that call," but I remained silent. In revitalization work, you will bump up against fiefdoms like this, and left unchallenged, they will keep the church from moving forward. In a worst-case scenario, the church will split. When fiefdoms take hold in an area, this encourages disputes to build over time. Ignoring fiefdoms as a leader only empowers the gatekeeper to keep pushing others away. When a new person tries to help the gatekeeper, instead of welcoming them, the gatekeeper feels threatened and chases the help away. Sometimes, the gatekeeper does this through ignoring or even being rude to the person offering support, which creates friction between the gatekeeper, helper, and pastoral leader. Addressing disputes is the first step in cutting off the power of the gatekeeper. Let's be honest—no one likes to have those hard conversations, but the gatekeeper keeps Christ out, and challenging discussions move Christ back in and egos out.

A gatekeeper uses disruption because they want to throw off the normal flow of the service or the inner workings of the church so that the leader comes to them to solve the issue. Typically, the disruption will enable the gatekeeper to gain valuable time or even look like the hero. But I have wondered: Who is the gatekeeper hurting when they try to stop the church's work by disrupting the normal flow in the church because someone is encroaching on their territory? Ultimately, they are hurting their relationship with God. I am not sure they always see it that way. What I have learned is that when you disrupt the opposing forces, you reinstall God at the center of the church and not man.

For God's Glory

For seven weeks, I was distracted by the delays and kept praying, hoping, and wondering whether the codes would be shared and whether the work would ever get accomplished. I even brought in a third-party church-board member to help defuse the situation. Still, even that backfired, because he chose not to share any information gleaned from the conversation except for handing me a sheet of paper with the codes on it. Even then, he never spoke. He just walked up, gave me the codes, and turned around. The flesh in me wanted to yell at the top of my lungs, but I could not allow the devil's distraction to get me caught up in emotions. Instead, I just prayed and released it to God. That very night, twenty-five teens poured their hearts out at the altar at the church, and God in that one moment reminded me that the church is in a spiritual battle against forces we cannot see, but God will win in the end. Since the fiefdom was taken down, the church member now sits in the lobby, refusing to enter the sanctuary, and then goes home after church with his family. In a way, it is his silent protest he thinks is against me, but it is really against God. How many people have come into a church intending it to be their church home, only to be run off by the gatekeepers of the church? Too many churches that are healthy looking on the outside are filled with sick members on the inside.

Challenging and busting through the gates of fiefdoms is not easy, but it is needed if God's church will be God's church. Churches controlled by carnal members and not Christlike followers will tear down and divide the church until there is nothing left. The only one who gets glory in a dying or dead church is the evil one. Pastors cannot be afraid to take a stand for God's house. If a person or family leaves because of the stand, then bless them and release them. You cannot control them, but you can manage your ability to help the church move forward in Christ.

Do yourself a favor. Do your church a favor. Overrun fiefdoms and take back the territory for God's glory.

5

The Community Is Waiting

Over eighty years ago, a missionary traveled to the island nation of Jamacia and began to share his faith with those he encountered. As he approached a small, dilapidated house with a dirt floor, he could see chickens running around in the yard and hear the laughter of children playing off in the distance. He was viewed through the owner's suspicious eyes, which were peering out from a small garden next to the house. Later, God would soften the man's heart to listen to the missionary, which would change his family's life forever.

One of the children from that family would grow up faith filled and on fire for God. This woman, Roslyn Burey, would first move to Canada and then the United States and begin attending church in a small town in Southwest Florida after she retired. In her late sixties, she was the church's mission president, sharing her passion with others.

It was in this church that I captured the vision and mission mindset, all because a missionary shared his faith with a family decades before. Through that prism of understanding, the passion for missions has taken hold, and it has become my driving force inside the local church. Over the years, three simple words—"connect,"

The Community Is Waiting

"serve," and "go"—have become the missional DNA that I see more and more churches needing.

There is no question that God has a plan and purpose for the local church. He has equipped her to be a beacon of hope in a world that is becoming increasingly challenging and more hostile to the gospel. God is resourcing his church to become the beachhead for missional outreach worldwide and in the local neighborhood in which the church serves. What is the vision that God has for your local church? For many churches, it is different depending on context and local needs. Where is God already working in the community? Where are your members serving or donating to in the community? Find ways to come alongside your members and the organizations they support and connect with the vision. Far too many churches try to develop programs that duplicate services in the community. God wants the church to use its resources to expand upon ministries and the gospel footprint, not compete. Connecting with the vision that God has for your church is relating to the community's needs holistically by resourcing all that the body has to give to help make the community better over the long term. Did you catch that? I did not say "one and done." Investing in your local community should be done through a long-term plan.

If you want to serve your community, spend some time driving around your community and seeing the needs around you. View the world as Christ would see it. Where do the lost hang out? Who is struggling to seek help? What organization is serving the underprivileged? As you are driving around, begin to take in the church's mission field and ask God in prayer where he wants the church to begin. See it as an opportunity to serve the community right where the greatest need is in the shadow of the steeple. Serve others as the hands and feet of Christ with love, grace, and understanding. With limited resources and people power, the promises of Christ can infiltrate the DNA of your church and transform her overnight into a missional community.

Through pastoral prayers, sermons, mentoring, and leadership development, you can begin to change the church's missional promise. It may take time, but God will begin to place the right

Addition through Subtraction

people in the right situations to lead these ministry teams into the community if you hold onto the promise.

As a leader who has a passion for helping the church be more like the community, you have probably heard, "Pastor, I just do not know what to do." What a unique opportunity to help your members become the missionaries God is commissioning your church to be. It is never too late to do something, but do something even if it fails, as there will be a life/spiritual lesson found. Christ has called the church to "go, make Christ-like disciples in the nations" (Matt 28:19), but far too many churches have chosen not to help the need next door, much less the nations. While the word has challenged the church for centuries to go, it seems that more and more say no. It is in this context that the DNA of the church has to be transformed by willing hearts, prayerful spirits, dedicated hands, and Christ's direction.

I can hear you now: "My people barely make it to church twice a month." The going part of the mission may be hard at first, but God will provide the people to lead and participate in these missional endeavors over time. At one time, the local church you serve in was a mission field; that is why it was planted. While you might never know why the church turned inward, you have an opportunity to lead them outward by strategizing, developing a team, and leading the first team into the community.

Over time, by connecting, serving, and going, the members will begin to become what God has called them to be. Think about is this way: the church that seemed destined for decay and closure will become a missional community center in all aspects. As the pastor, you can help change the church's DNA by leading them forward, but are you willing?

Do Not Be Afraid to Minister in the Shadows

As Rachel[1] shares her story, she pauses and stares off into space, her eyes fixated on what is unseen. She blinks fast as she gets back

---

1. Not her real name.

to telling me how since the young age of twelve, she has been using some form of narcotic. While it started on a whim, it has become her daily reality. Everything she has done from that moment on has been about chasing the next fix that her body yearns for. The effects of that decision from decades ago have left her with paralysis down her left side, the lingering effects of an overdose. Even when her body began to fail her, she still sought the next fix to ease her anxious mind.

I am not sure we will ever know why some people do what they do, but I know this: the Rachels of this world still need a warm meal and a kind word. They still need dignity offered to them. They still need a hand up. Your community and most church families have felt the sting of a "Rachel" in their family—a person who has been loved and cared for yet still wanders down a path of self-destruction.

As for Rachel, she is trying. She has been clean for two weeks, was recently baptized at a local church, and is doing her best to turn her life around. Her body may still carry the past scars, but through hope, she will find healing. Each day, Rachel and many others come into the soup kitchen I run, not seeking judgment and harsh words but a meal and a safe place to rest for the moment. The program is more than just a meal; it is a life buoy that provides a small glimmer of hope for a drowning soul. God has called his church to minister to those in the shadows of his steeple.

God is calling the church to turn toward people who live on the margins of society. The marginalized have become hidden in plain view. Today, the church needs to begin reaching out to those cast aside by the modern gadgets which have replaced relationships with devices and a lack of connectedness. In every community, there is a neighborhood or portion of town where the shadows gather away from the view of other community members. There is no doubt in my mind that it is in these areas that Jesus can be found today if a church is willing to venture into the outer regions. I feel in my spirit that the church is being called back to the shadows to minister to the homeless, addicted, and those struggling with mental illness. Churches are strategically placed

Addition through Subtraction

in kingdom opportunities to serve the needy. For many churches, the work starts by acknowledging the need, seeing the conditions, and praying about meeting that need. What can you do? How can you help?

Every day, the same number of minutes is given to each of us. How a person uses those minutes tells a lot about what they care about and what their priorities are in life. The life span of many churches is about eighty years. When you evaluate the amount of time that members throughout the decades have invested in their community, the church falls short in real kingdom advancement most of the time. I am not a math whiz, but I did name this book *Addition through Subtraction*, so hang in there with me. Suppose every church member has 86,400 seconds to the day. Can a member find a way to serve? The simple answer is yes. Throughout the New Testament, we see men and women who served by advancing the message of Christ by going to the margins of communities to seek the lost and broken. Ministering in the shadows is about investing time in some of the darkest places of the community. It is walking where sin is alive. What matters is that Christ's love can conquer.

Again, pause and reflect: Where is God at work in your community? What community organization is already meeting the needs of those living in the shadows? Find that place and serve. How many churches spend minutes—not even hours—of their day living out the gospel beyond group gatherings inside the four walls of the church? If I can spend an average of seven hours a day on my devices, according to my Apple phone, I can find an hour a week to serve in the community. Serving in the shadows is about helping where the church can. Maybe it is not serving a meal at a soup kitchen but collecting clothing for the local clothing closet, establishing an after-school enrichment program in the church's basement, or opening the doors of the church on a hot or cold day to provide comfort to those who need extra care. Serving those in the shadows is more about being the hands and feet of Jesus than starting a program. It is showing God's love.

Do yourself a favor when you drive through the community or step outside the church's doors: see Jesus in every face you encounter. Christ lives in the shadows within your community. When the church sees Jesus in its neighbors, the church starts to see where Jesus is calling her. Many Rachels need a Jesus-loving church that lives out her faith seven days a week and not just on Sunday. God is calling his people back to the community to minister to those in the shadows. Will your church be one of them?

Transformational Community Connections

Over the decades, the way the church had been framed has changed. In decades past, all the church had to do was open its doors, and the community would come. The people were preconditioned to the idea that twice on Sunday and once on Wednesday night, it was church time. Fast-forward two decades into a new century, and that spiritual calling seems backward to many in today's society. So, what happened? There has been a transformational culture shift, and it has infiltrated the church. The church is no longer the center of social and community welfare, as it once was. The church can no longer be seen as "come and visit" but "go and serve." With a societal shift away from traditional worship attendance being counted three times weekly, the church has to lean into this new era of the transformational promise they find themselves in to connect with the neighborhood around them in new and creative ways. For decades, the established church subtracted, because she was unwilling or unable to reach the neighborhood around the church property, partly because of the community decline related to a host of factors and partly because the people had decided to hunker down and try to ride the slide out. These once-grand buildings built decades before sat like silos waiting for the people to return. That time has come. A new generation of Christ followers is moving back to the city, where they can work, play, and live all in one place. What an opportunity for the established church to reconnect with those they once lost.

Addition through Subtraction

Will the Church Do the Work?

As the church transitions into a new season of her life, she has a unique opportunity to develop community partnerships with organizations that impact the community in ways that the church could only dream of. There is a tendency in the established church to retread programs from what worked in the past. You cannot repeat the past and have a healthy outcome. Look for new opportunities in your daily routine. I have found that many nonprofit organizations need and want volunteers who are willing to donate their time, talents, and treasures to help the worthy cause. Instead of reinventing the wheel, the church should develop ties with community partners to support the nonprofit and strengthen the local church. Let us be the church. You have heard it said that "the church is not a building; it is the people." Well, be the people who serve the community and live out your faith calling as a church.

There is a propensity for a declining church to do one-and-done events out in the community and believe that it will be the one thing that brings people back to church. When it does not happen and the disappointment sets in, the church declares, "The community does not care about us, so why should we care about them?" Subtraction did not happen overnight. Give yourself permission not to die by the attendance numbers. Rather than seeing these events as one-and-done outreach events, the church must know that these community engagements are where discipleship can take place by sharing the gospel in ways not typically done weekly. When this happens, these community outreaches take on a new perceptive and life of their own. The church begins to look more like Jesus than a social club—creating a safe space where the church and neighborhood connect, counsel, and encourage each other while the church is serving the community through biblically based living. Over time, this type of engagement may warm some hearts, and in return, they may want to come to be a part of the neighborhood church that serves the community.

In the end, transformational community connections are about developing a place where the community and church can

The Community Is Waiting

connect outside the norms of a traditional church service. This is where outreach becomes the platform for future addition. I have seen addition come through clothing closets, feeding programs, afterschool enrichment classes, adult education classes, and a host of other formats. Look around the neighborhood. Ask yourself: Where are the poor, the broken, and the hurting? That is where the church is needed the most. Go where your people will be uncomfortable and serve. By serving in the margins, the challenging places become God's place where you can share about Christ and grow spiritually. It may not feel natural at first, but when the neighborhood sees that the church cares, they will care about the church. It is only then that the hearts of the lost, broken, and addicted will be open to hearing the heart-holiness message that the church has to share.

The decline in your local church has not happened overnight and will not correct itself in a short time frame. Instead, it will take a sustained effort on the church's part to keep serving the community even when the fruit is unseen. God is calling you and the established church to reconnect and stay connected with the community in which she lives. Sustained effort over a prolonged time will bring fruit if the church is willing to not give up easily. I grew up in Southwest Florida, where Thomas Edison, one of the inventors of the light bulb, had a winter home and laboratory. Standing just inside his laboratory, I was able to view the space where he tried and failed over one thousand times before he perfected the light bulb.[2] Since then, the light bulb has been redesigned and reimaged in ways that even Edison would be surprised at, but he would still recognize the concept of the effort.

The community needs your church. But it requires a church that is focused not only on Sunday mornings but on Jesus. I challenge you to pick up the mantle and become the neighborhood church for the community.

---

2. I say one of the inventors, as Edison was part of a series of inventors who worked to develop the modern light bulb. See Matulka and Wood, "Light Bulb."

6

Leading to Future Victories

In January of 2019, I arrived at my current assignment with excitement and anticipation for what God would do. In a way, I was coming home to Appalachia, and I was ready to reconnect with roots built over the years serving in her mountainous arms as a pastor. The first year, it seemed like everything I did had an anointing, leading to growth in attendance, baptisms, membership, new believers, families with children, and the list could go on. The honeymoon was sweet and gave me space to enjoy what God was doing. Year two was a rude awakening as I moved from enjoying serving to navigating uncharted territory brought on by a pandemic. The once-vibrant campus I pastored became a ghost town as she closed physically for four months. When the church reopened, it saw a decline in membership, loss of many of the young families, staff leaving to new assignments, and financial hardship brought on by the lack of giving. The honeymoon, which was so sweet, moved toward divorce with the rude awakening that what had been was no longer, and the pain set in.

When the church was growing and reaching new people, the negative voices upset over the change inside the church were muted and moved to the background. But year two exposed the freshness of the change. The reality of a once-in-a-generation pandemic

Leading to Future Victories

exposed the fault lines that were hidden as growth took hold. Now the church was fighting strong headwinds on two fronts: the negative voices and the decline caused by the pandemic.

According to Thom Rainer, years two through five are some of the most challenging years in ministry. Many pastors and churches do not make it out of years two through five because of all the pushbacks. Year one (stage one) is the honeymoon year (and if you are lucky, it will move into year two). Years two through five (stages two and three) are tactical battles for the heart and soul of the church. It is spiritual guerilla warfare. Years six through ten (stage four) are traditionally growth years driven by people who have settled into the church's vision. Years eleven and beyond (stage five) are seen for many leaders as a new crossroads—confronting new problems or becoming complacent.[1] So, what does a pastor do to get to the big wins in ministry?

Looking for Wins

In a season of uncertainty, I always look for a quick win to stop the bleeding and to help turn things around. Even in a dire situation, there is always hope if you will pause, reflect, and then follow the Holy Spirit's guidance. God is saying to go after low-hanging fruit. For me, low-hanging fruit was redesigning directional signs and the worship card and developing a mission/vision wall that reinforced who we were becoming as a church. It reestablished a center for the church, showed the church that something new was happening, and focused those willing to adapt on the fact that the church was moving forward again.

The lapse of regular attendees due to the pandemic has shrunk the church. Where members usually attended regularly, they are now attending once or twice a month if the church is lucky. The lack of commitment to the local church has been demonstrated across all denominational lines and communities of faith, not just in the Church of the Nazarene. God is calling the church to quickly

---

1. Rainer, "Five Stages." See also Blackwell, "Church Health."

reengage with those who have been lost due to the comforts of staying home. There are several ways to reconnect with those lost: social media, phone calls, text messages, Messenger, postcards, and prayer, just to name a few resources that are free or close to free. There are so many times the church gets caught up in our needs and misses the people's needs. You have an excellent opportunity to pray for a family or individual who has not returned. Make them part of your prayer life. Let the families know you are praying. It will encourage their soul and plant seeds for a return.

People inside and outside the church have been watching how she bears the pandemic, mask mandate, politics, and community engagement through social media posts, up close as attendees, and through the gossip train that runs across town. The church has been living in crisis mode for two years. Plus, the pandemic has led to a constant leadership fatigue which can lead to failure as a leader. Evaluate how you have handled the challenges that the church has faced. Pastor, God has called you to be decisive and deliberate in your leadership style. I did not say to be brash and arrogant but to make "God choices" over "faction choices." Be Christ in your leadership, and be compassionate in your words. Remember that people are watching. The vision God gave you for the church most likely has changed, as a culture shift has occurred. Let me encourage you to begin to dream again by learning the new needs of the church, sharing what you learn, and reinforcing the vision that God has given you as you point people to Jesus. God is not surprised by the challenges you face today in the church. He is not surprised by how church members can tear down others because they are living under stress. Do not get blinded by the world's abuse; keep your eyes on the vision that God has given the church, and trust in him always as you lead well.

Victory Is Coming

How many times have you gotten stuck because others have wanted to pull you back into the past? Let me encourage you to move on and move forward to the new day at hand. Do not linger too

Leading to Future Victories

long on the past. While you can learn a lot from the past, there is no need to rehash old battles that are not yours to fight. Keep moving forward by sharing the vision, winning small victories, and responding in love to those trying to hold the church back. The big-C church has lost two years of forward movement. It is time for the church to take back territory that the devil has a foothold in. It is time for the church to rise and claim victories, however small, inside the church. Look for the low-hanging fruit that wins can be built on. Begin to plan and execute that plan to rebuild God's kingdom one victory at a time.

I know deep inside my spirit that the church is a great place to celebrate what God is doing. Far too many members are quick to post a negative comment on social media or talk negatively about what is happening or not happening in the church. Let me give you a four-letter word. Ready? S-t-o-p! It is time to celebrate the "God things" happening in the life of the church. Celebrate corporately on Sunday morning. Celebrate in small groups. Celebrate in one-on-one conversations. Begin to turn negative conversations or whimsical look-backs into celebrating what's happening now. God is still working in the life of your church. He still has victories for the church, but we often only see the negative or hear the loudest voice in the room, instead of seeing God in the new family that visited, the remodeling of the nursery, or the telephone tree set up to take prayer requests.

It takes quick steps in God's direction to claim future victories in the life of your church revitalization. Be encouraged today; God sees your need, hears your prayers, and is moving things in your favor behind the scenes. Know this truth: a supernatural spiritual breakthrough is coming your church's way if you keep looking for quick wins, reengaging church members, responding to God's voice in your midst, sharing the vision, turning from the past or setbacks, and celebrating the successes in the life of your church.

Addition through Subtraction

Building Success through the Multiplication Effect

The reality is that that most churches are far too comfortable being comfortable. What do you do if you are leading a church that finds itself in a comfortable posture? Do you hear God? You are called to lead them out of conformity and into a future built upon prayer, plans, proposals, and praises. One of the things I enjoy the most about social media is watching other pastors and churches from afar and looking for strategies that can fit into my local context.

In the southern part of the United States, I admire one such pastor, Kevin McDonald. I even went so far as to pay him and the cofounder of the ministry group he led, Jeremiah Wood, to come to train my laypeople in a church that I pastored at the time. This allowed me to observe his methods up close. Over time, I witnessed a familiar pattern that I have dubbed the "multiplication effect." The formula (pray, plan, propose, and praise) is rudimentary at best, but highly effective over time. In my own ministry, I have tried implementing the multiplication effect and have seen added numerical, spiritual, and physical growth in the local church.

Established churches that fall into decline enter a cycle of weak prayers that are primarily focused inward on the church's problems and the people who gather each week. God has not created his church to be a weak church but instead to be bold prayer warriors for Christ who call upon heaven with desperation in anticipation of what God can do on behalf of them. Building success in the church is laying a foundation that is built on prayer. You want your church to grow? Pray. You want active families as part of the church? Pray. You want more resources to do ministry with? Pray. Without prayer, the church will perish. Prayer brings about honest reflections on what has happened, is happening, and will happen in the church's life. Develop a team of prayer warriors that will pray their spiritual guts out for Jesus—giving everything they have to the one who gave them everything. Prayer cannot be five minutes or less on a Sunday but intentional and relational times of corporate and individual prayer for needs inside and outside of the church several times a week. If the church is to move heaven with their prayers, they must be willing to push themselves into a position of prayer with a long-term lens.

Let's be honest: we often do not have the spiritual guts to pray bold prayers that lead to the revelation of big "God plans" for the church. Instead, we hide away, waiting for God, waiting for people to show up, and waiting for families with children over time. The God plan gets put on the shelf until finances get better, teens come, or a new building is built. Waiting becomes a barrier to God's plans. Sometimes, I wonder if God is just bored silly with all this waiting that his church does. God has called the church to step out in bold faith and claim the mantle he created them to achieve, not to hide and wait.

Reflect on your local church's past and present, but then dream about what the future could be. What is stopping the church from moving forward? Write it down; capture the thoughts. Now give it all over to God. Trust God! If God has given you/the church the dream, he will provide the provisions to accomplish the vision. Let me encourage you to dream and believe big.

Realize that when a church is struggling, one win is all that is needed to get back on track. You've probably been there yourself, as you hear the opposing viewpoints instead of positive affirmations about what is happening in the church. In a turnaround situation, the leader must be strategic in selecting low-hanging and multilayered projects as they move toward wins in the church. Low-hanging projects create initial successes that can be built upon to gather the much-needed momentum to tackle the larger projects in the future. So, look around. What is the low-hanging fruit that you can capture? In my current assignment, low-hanging fruit was redoing signage, which led to freshening up the welcome area, paving the parking lot, fellowship expansion, and youth-wing addition. One little step sparked more significant and extensive efforts, until we began to tackle some of the God dreams that the church has had. With excitement in the air, members invite others to attend and then participate in the church, and growth begets growth over time.

As God moves, praise him. I love to praise and celebrate what God is doing in the church. I take to social media, personal conversations, and my writing to tell people what God is doing in my life and the local church. Why? Because it is not me who is doing these things but God. As the church gleans low-hanging fruit, wins begin to develop, and there is a tendency for the pastor to be viewed as the conquering hero when the pastor has only obeyed God. Turning the praise from the pastor to the Savior is a component of good leadership and reinforces that God is the one in control and not the church. When my local church tips the pizza-delivery driver as part of our blessing day at church twice a year, with a large tip for one pizza, we celebrate with praise and prayer. The church knows that we would not be able to do it without God generously giving to us beyond our means. On these special days, I love watching the people come forward, dropping off cash in an offering bucket at the feet of the delivery driver, and each time we have done it, the driver shared a story of how much they needed the funds. Why do we do it? To celebrate the generosity and love of Christ with a stranger and to tell the person that even strangers love them. Find creative and innovative ways to bless total strangers and watch how that brings your church alive.

God has a perfect plan for your local church, and through a series of simple steps (pray, plan, propose, and praise), he is willing to partner with your local church to do extraordinary things for the kingdom.

Celebrating a Parking Lot

In 2012, the church began dreaming of a new place to worship. For over a half century, the traditional-looking church served near the same spot, but on that day, they were embarking on a whole new journey. For many churches, when they reach an advanced age, they begin to die. It seemed far-fetched that a church at the end of her life cycle would give birth again. Yet, the leaders believed that resetting her life span by building anew would save the church in the future. Two years later, on Father's Day 2014, the church gathered to unveil a brand-new, modern building. With excitement in the air, the church moved in and began to grow again. Over time, the forward momentum was lost after the pastor left within a year of moving into the new building. The next pastor the church hired only stayed two years before he relocated for his wife's work. In 2019, when I became the church's pastor, they had a beautiful building, but dreams were left unattained. The board dreamed of paving the gravel parking lot, expanding the fellowship hall, dividing the upstairs into separate youth and children's wings, creating new signage, and supporting local and international missions.

In one of the earliest conversations about the parking lot, the board expressed its belief that if we paved the parking lot, people would come. Can I be honest with you? I thought that was the silliest thing I had ever heard. A parking lot would bring people into the church. That sounded too questionable to me, yet this was the people's dream, and I set aside my doubts and trusted the God dream. The estimates we gathered for the paving were high, but we trusted that God would provide the $70,000 to complete the parking lot. Through limited resources and a twenty-four-month loan, we paved the parking lot. Lo and behold, people began to come. And not just any people, but families with children. Our children's program flourished, and the increase in tithes enabled us to pay budgets in full for only the second time in twenty years, paying off $70,000 worth of debt in two years.

Then the pandemic hit, and the number of families with children was cut in half, offerings all but collapsed, I took a 25 percent pay cut, and part-time staff either became volunteers or voluntarily cut their pay. A board member donated $5,000 to pay some of our bills, and we took a government-backed loan. What had looked hopeful just a year before turned sour fast. Where families had once filled the parking lot, there were now more empty spots than cars. Did I think about giving up? Maybe for a few minutes, but inside of me, I could not. There was too much on the line. Spiritual lives, for one. The church's legacy was teetering on death, and the board and I were determined to see the church through this crisis

Addition through Subtraction

or at least to give it our best try. By making bold decisions to revamp how and when we did church, we weathered the storm.

Each Sunday from my office window, I look out over the parking lot and remember the early victory. I claim that victory. I talk about that victory. I walk that victory out as I pick up trash around the parking lot, thanking God for showing me what could happen if I tangibly trust him. So, amid the pandemic storm, I trusted him, believing by faith that the God who provided a parking lot could do it again. At the time of me writing this book, we are still slowly bouncing back from our pandemic low, but I still hear God saying to aim high each time I look at the parking lot. Let me encourage you to claim a victory, big or small, and to remember that God still has a victory for the church ahead.

7

Living in a Spirit of Service

As the music began to play softly, I could sense in my spirit that it was time to commit to God's calling on my life. While I knew for years that God was calling me into ministry, it was at this moment that I felt like I needed to decide to either follow him or the world, but I could not have both. That day, I attended a district prayer and fasting service in the Southern Florida District and knew God's pull on my heart succinctly. As the worship team played "I Surrender All," I felt the warming in my spirit and the inner voice that said, "Give it all to me now." I began white-knuckling the chair in front of me, not wanting to go forward, but I felt the Holy Spirit's presence over me and slowly walked to the altar as tears welled up in my eyes. As I bent down to pray, the floodgates of emotion overwhelmed me as warm tears streamed down my cheeks and a heavy burden was lifted from me. At the altar, I gave my life not only to God but also to the Church of the Nazarene. I did not know then what lay ahead, but I knew who would be at the head of my life, guiding me each step of the way.

While others would soon question my calling, I knew beyond a shadow of a doubt that God had called me, and I had fully surrendered to his will for my life and future ministry. God's calling has sustained me through some harsh days and glorious celebrations throughout the years. Even as I write these words, I wonder what would have happened if I had not truly understood the calling on my life and ignored what he was saying to me? What about you? Do you know the calling on your life? If you know the why behind the calling, you have the key that unlocks the purpose for your life. If you do not know who you serve, why you serve, and where you serve, I guarantee you that you will get to a place where you will walk away from ministry disgusted by the actions of those connected to the church. Serving God is more than just standing in a pulpit and sharing a message; it is a life fully committed to him.

Whom Do You Serve?

Think back to the last time you sat at a church-board table preparing your heart, mind, and soul for the questions that would be asked by members who formed the church search committee. While polity dictates specific steps in calling a pastor, you need to remember that the Holy Spirit guides the process. Carnal individuals have tried to remove the Spirit of God from the process in the past, but God always wins out by guiding the board and pastoral candidate into a relationship that he sees fit. Sometimes, it is a call to the church, and other times it is away from the church. Serving God is all about fully committing yourself to his will, direction, and calling on your life.

Why Do You Serve?

Be honest with yourself: the past two years have been rough. You had to make decisions on the fly, mediate between warring mask factions, and navigate political and personal minefields, all while watching a portion of your congregation leave the church and never return. In this season of uncertainty, the idea of giving up or moving to the next church has had to cross your mind at least once. So, what keeps you serving where you are? Hopefully, you were able to say God. If it is people, programs, or property, that can all be taken away in a flash—or, in this case, a pandemic.

Think about it this way: It is not by accident that you serve in your current assignment. God has called you to lead your people faithfully by preaching his word, disciplining, and helping people strengthen their relationship with Christ through a personal walk with him. It is not your job to read the tea leaves, so leave all of that alone and love people as Christ has loved you. Forgive people as Christ has forgiven you. Be the pastor your people need you to be. Be more like Christ.

Where Do You Serve?

I sometimes sit in the church parking lot and stare at the building where I pastor. I never really thought about it, but it must be an odd sight to see someone sitting in their car looking at a church. Maybe those who pass by do not pay that much attention to someone sitting and staring. The truth is, I usually am talking to God. In this time of reflecting, I think about previous pastors—the decisions they had to make, the dreams that did not come to fruition, and the promises that God has revealed to me for this time in the church's life. I have taken one nugget of truth from countless stare visits: my church address and location are not there by accident. A church planter or committee selected the site, guided by the Holy Spirit to reach a specific geographic area with the gospel. While you may think your address is an accident, it is instead a divine revelation by God. It truly is holy ground. Let me say that again: your address is a divine revelation from God. Yes, the place that at times drives you crazy has been divinely planted to reach the lost, broken, and hurting with the gospel of grace, hope, and love, and you have a significant part to play.

What you do matters, pastor. Who, why, and where is essential to the God story that is being written through your ministry. The next time you feel you want to give up, think back to your calling, the moment of surrender, and then recommit to serving him as a small gesture of thankfulness for God serving you through Jesus.

Addition through Subtraction
Staying Faithful in the "Why Not?"

A pastor shared with me, "Why has God put me in this godforsaken place?" Before I judged him, I paused and reflected on the sentiments shared in his statement. Parishioners might see the pastor's job as "easy," not realizing the hours put into shepherding the flock behind the scenes and pouring themselves into their calling behind every sermon. Many times, the pastor is bitten by the ones the pastor is called to love. The struggle of staying faithful in service to the church is challenging but rewarding.

It is predicted that more churches will open over the next decade than there will be pastors to fill pulpits. Just in the past month, I have spoken to three denominational leaders who have a total of fourteen churches open and are seeking candidates. Instead of asking, "Why, God?" what about asking, "Why not, God?" God, why not help me stand in the calling by staying put? God, why not send me to where the mission is? God, why not keep pouring out your love on me so I can pour it on others? God, why not let me trust you with my calling? When a pastor shares the sentiments of a struggle, the revitalizer needs to realize that they are in the winter of discontent, but that spring is coming. It is in the darkness that God begins to pierce with light, and the revitalizer finds direction in the light, which allows the "Why not?" to become "Thank you, God." Before the pandemic, the average pastor stayed just over three and a half years, which means that half the pastors left before and after that allotted period. Across all denominations, the pandemic has accelerated pastoral transitions through retirement, staff reduction, and relocation.

Now more than ever, the church needs pastors who will stand in their calling and stay put. That might be the pot calling the kettle black when you look at my resume, but I am personally committed to staying where God has called me until God moves me from that local church. The church is bleeding members, money, and mission. Think about it this way. What a great time for the pastoral leader to stand up and begin to cast a fresh vision for the local church by helping lead the people forward. While a pastor may not

Living in a Spirit of Service

add people through charm and personality, the pastor can help the people lay the foundational squares to revitalization and rebuilding through prayer, biblical teaching/preaching, and functionally preparing for guests. When the church is subtracting members rather than adding, starting a new program, or investing limited resources in a new project, this may not be wise stewardship of God's funds, so what can a church do? Throughout the local community, organizations are doing a tremendous job reaching the needs of the lost. Go to where God is already at work and get working with God. Five days a week, I work as the executive director of a community pantry and soup kitchen that primarily focuses on the homeless population and those living in poverty. From ordering food to paying bills, serving food, and more, I live on mission each day. Stop for a moment and reflect. Where can you or the church be on mission?

We all want the local church to grow, but if we are not willing to invest our time in the community, why should God invest in a social club called the church? I know that may sound harsh, but the church needs the community, and the community needs the church to be its best self, sending selfless Christ followers into her fields. Find a mission in the community where your skill sets and needs can be used the most and serve. From community boards, reading to children in schools, or helping the homeless, there are community groups that need your church's support not only in dollars but in time.

When the world seems to be going off a cliff, the world needs a church that embraces her with open arms and an unfailing commitment to be like Jesus. Let me encourage you to pour out Jesus upon the remaining members who have not walked away. Pour out Jesus upon the community, which desperately needs a loving and kind church. Pour out Jesus in your personal and professional life. It is not by accident but by divine appointment that you are living through a modern-day pandemic. See the pandemic and the remnants of it not as a negative but as an opportunity to live out your faith daily. While you may grieve those who have not returned, take a stand to pour out Christ upon those who have remained.

Addition through Subtraction

When the church is down and out, get out of the four walls. Serve like Christ. Serve the community like never before and watch how God blesses the investment in others.

Think about it this way: when trouble comes, you must trust God's timing. I get it; this is a tough season in the life of the church. As you mount the stage every Sunday and your eyes scan the crowd, you can see who has left and not returned, but hear my heart—trust God's timing. God has the right people before you in this pruning season, and he is preparing to send reinforcements. Will he find your leadership faithful or faltering? My hope is that you remain faithful. In due time, the floodgates of heaven will open, and new people and families will come to the church, but you have to do your part. You have to lead with a God vision. You have to inspire the people not merely in words but in deeds. You have to be an example of God's grace and extend love to the outcasts of society. The most incredible days for God's church are ahead, not behind.

As you wait, be willing to fully surrender to God's plan for your ministry and to be faithful in the small things. God is going to bless it.

Three Ways to Grind It Out for God

It had been a few weeks since I walked on the treadmill at the gym. Halfway through my walk, I felt tired, wanting to give up, watching the clock, and dreading every minute of the uphill climb. Doesn't that sound like the church today? You started the year with high hopes, only to face the headwinds of a pandemic and problems related to how the church and her people reacted. It got me thinking about serving in the established church during one of the most challenging seasons in the church's life. I am hearing more and more pastors wanting to give up or walking away altogether. Maybe that is you today. You might not see hope and find yourself in a season of discouragement. Let me encourage you to not give up but to grind it out for God. I get it. I do. This season is sucking the spiritual and physical life out of your ministry. You may feel you cannot win; either way, stress levels are up and discouragement abounds, but ask: God, did you call me to give up? Unless you are near the retirement age or have lost your calling, I want to encourage you to grind it out one service, one prayer, one teaching at a time, because God is not done with your ministry yet.

Grind for a Win

If you have ever lived in an industrial city, you have seen the black clouds hanging over the landscape, blocking out the sun, and felt the soot against your skin. As you breathed, you might have felt the heaviness in your lungs as you took in the adverse effects that came from the progress of a modern society.

Inside the four walls of the established church, there can be the soot of negative feelings, bewilderment, and heaviness that blocks out any progress. When discouragement takes hold in the leadership, it begins to choke out the positive effects of what is being done and has been done in the church's life. Instead of embracing the dark forces, embrace the Sonship of Christ. Look for the wins that he has brought about. You might say, "There are no wins!" There are always wins in the church's life, but sometimes, you need a little reminder. Wins are examples of God's movement in the life of the church. Sometimes, wins are the bulletins printed weekly, but they can be as large as someone coming to Christ. A win helps redirect the focus from the negative to the positive.

Think about it this way. If your ship were capsized by a large wave and you were swept into the water, you would immediately look for the shore, or at least something to hold onto. So, too, when trying to keep your head above water in a revitalization work, you swim to things that can lift you—one positive comment, one service done well, one life radically changed—to restore your spiritual confidence.

Addition through Subtraction

Grind for a New Definition of Success

What is the story that plays over and over in your head? The story of lack? The story of loss? The story of "What if?"? We all have played the stories of "What if we had a newer building?" "What if we had children?" "What if we had more teens?" You can play the "What if?" game all you want, but it will not change your circumstances. So, what will? The simple answer is God. But the long and short of it is changing your definition of success. For far too long, the idea of success has been measured not by church health, spiritual growth, or touchpoints in the community but through numerical gains—more importantly, bottoms in the seats. While counting people is one way to measure growth, it does not measure the church's spiritual health. Too many "growing" churches before the pandemic have shrunk significantly, because the people counted as "members" were not truly invested in the church. Remember: success can be as small as having a greeter at the door, a Sunday School teacher willing to teach, or baptizing someone for the first time in several years. To succeed in God's eyes is to be ready to serve in the place God has called you. To love people that may not love you. To embrace the challenges of the season you find yourself in and to keep moving forward despite the challenges.

Grind for a Renewed Passion

When ministry begins to get tough, it can steal the joy of serving in the local church. For over twenty-four months, the church has been hammered by a pandemic, politics, and personalities associated with the fractionalization of the world. For the longest time, the church was a haven from society's ills. Over time, the church retreated from the world, and now the forces of darkness are pushing against the compound where the church hides each Wednesday and Sunday. Instead of retreating even further, look at it this way: what an opportunity to reconnect with the world by becoming Christ to the community around the church. Regardless of where you are located, there are areas in your community

Living in a Spirit of Service

that need people to invest in them. It can be a community project such as painting a park bench, picking up trash, or feeding the homeless. Wherever the need, God is already there, waiting on his people to invest.

The passion you want or need to have for the church only comes through a solid personal relationship with Jesus Christ. Christ taught throughout his word that he wants to use his church to accomplish kingdom advancement, and he needs the church to surrender willfully. Will you be someone who leaves God's passion for your own? Or will you lead with a renewed passion for the lost? If you say yes, it starts with you praying, reading his word, listening to what he has to say, and obeying his will for your life and the local church. There will be a day when this season of hardship will pass, but will you still be holding on to the Son to see it come? Only you know that answer, but let me encourage you to keep being your best and leave the rest to God.

So, after reflecting on this chapter, can you answer the question "Whom do you serve?" Whatever the answer, spend some time confirming your calling with God. Find time alone to pray, reflect, and write what God is saying to you. The next part of your ministry is going to be incredible if you do. If you don't, it could lead to a period of disappointment and heartache. Stay strong, friend. God still has more for you to do with your ministry.

8

What Drives You to Help Lead the Church

I WAS HALFWAY THROUGH the master's program at Trevecca Nazarene University when it finally dawned on me: data had to become the driving force of my ministry after following the Holy Spirit, or I would live in a self-focused ministry mindset and not in the Savior's calling. That epiphany (data-driven leadership) shined a light in an area where I was weak. Let that sink in. That is a significant shift. Data is the second most crucial thing that you can understand in the church, behind the gifting of the Holy Spirit. Before I lose you, I know you might not rank it that high, but hear my heart—it is essential. If you are going to help lead a turnaround in your local congregation, you must know your community and adjacent areas better than anyone else. That makes data-driven decision-making a significant milestone in a turnaround church. Understanding the data enables you as a leader to drive discussions at the board table not just on a whim but with factual information that will help the church narrow its focus and deliver the best bang for the spiritual buck.

The Church of the Nazarene has a research arm that collects, then correlates, data on worship attendance, baptism, communion, etc. If you want to understand where a church stands compared to other churches, the research arm of the global church most likely has the data you need to review. If you belong to another denomination, you will have a similar research arm, but it may not be a research center. Ask around; someone is collecting and correlating the data. Every year as a pastor, I fill out a pastoral report for my denomination, and I never really thought about what happened to the data. To make the best decision, you need real-time data. I do not want to geek out or lose you, so I will keep this chapter short and sweet, but I want to provide you with a line of thinking that you can evaluate and possibly use in your local context.

Since you are eight chapters into this book, one can assume your church needs church revitalization, or the church is currently going through church revitalization, and that is why you bought this book in the first place. Maybe you were looking for the one silver bullet to solve your church's problems. By now, you must realize that it is not one thing alone that can or will turn around the church, but a series of things done over a long period of time that begins to turn the tide of decline. Without accurate real-time data, you might be trying something that does not fit your context, hampering your revitalization efforts and forcing the church closer to death. So, let's look at the data from a thirty-thousand-foot level by using the data that comes directly from pastoral reports within the Church of the Nazarene, and then let's drill down to get closer to your local church. If you are a non-Nazarene reading this portion of the book, it might not seem relevant. But hold on—do not skip ahead. You might find it helpful to compare the data to your local church's or denomination's data, which will help you see what is happening across the broader church in North America.

Understand Your Size

Anytime I am around another pastor, we try to ease into the conversation of "How big is your church?" I do not want the other pastor to think that is all I care about, but it is one sign of a healthy church. That thinking was negatively set in stone in 2014 when

Addition through Subtraction

my wife and I were invited to the Order of the Flame, a gathering of leaders within the Wesleyan Methodist family of churches to which the Church of the Nazarene belongs. I was pastoring a church of about fifty-five people and was excited to meet and learn from others in the global Wesleyan tree that I was a part of. There were only five of us who were Nazarene pastors at the event, so it was natural for us to gravitate toward one another in such a large group. However, I learned in a rather abrupt way that size matters to some pastors. Three of us were in churches with less than sixty people, while two were in larger churches ranging from 135 to four-hundred-plus members. Once the two pastors who had larger churches heard our numbers, subconsciously or on purpose, the pastors ignored us the remainder of the time. It hurt that we were rejected for serving our local church. At that event on St. Simons Island, Georgia, I promised God that if I ever had the opportunity to serve at a larger church, I would be an encourager to pastors at smaller churches and not look down upon them.

In 2017, 75 percent of Church of the Nazarene churches in North America had on average less than one hundred people each Sunday for worship. When you drill down into those numbers, you realize the church is a lot smaller than those initial numbers indicate. About forty-seven percent (47.3 percent) of Church of the Nazarene churches in 2017 had less than fifty people.[1] Think about it this way: nearly half of the Church of the Nazarene churches in North America had less than fifty people each Sunday in 2017, so where do you fit? Most likely, in this category as an average-sized church. I was serving in a normal-sized church in 2014, and I thought I was a small-church pastor when my local church was on target with other churches across North America. Revitalizers, learn from my misthinking—do not let your thoughts negatively affect your self-worth, because, in reality, you are serving where God wants you to help. In the most recent data (2019–20), the average size (a church of fifty or less) has ticked slightly up to 48.7 percent (2019) and 50 percent (2020).[2] If you fall into

---

1. Laura K. Lance, email message to author, March 16, 2022.
2. Laura K. Lance, email message to author, August 5, 2021.

this category, let me shout it at the top of my lungs: You are in *a normal-sized church*! Okay, I feel much better. Do you? Simply put, you are doing better than you realize. Your church matters to God, and he sees what you are accomplishing in the revitalization effort. Be proud of your calling. Be proud of your work. Be proud of your church. You are on target.

Keep the Church Doors Open

In a survey sampling of Church of the Nazarene district superintendents, my colleague Dr. Paul Hobbs sought firsthand assessments from varied district leaders in North America. As I reviewed the data with Dr. Hobbs, it was staggering in the sense that district leadership sees the need for church revitalization. Still, there is no central, educational revitalization institution to lead revitalization-training efforts for the denomination. The Southern Baptist Convention and the Assemblies of God have clearly defined courses, degrees, and schools that address this issue. While I advocate for Nazarene Bible College to lead this effort, as they are training and graduating more pastors for ministry within the Church of the Nazarene, it could also take on a regional approach where the regional Nazarene universities in the United States collaborate together to develop and train churches in the area of church revitalization.

Let me turn to the data that Dr. Hobbs accumulated and offer the raw data and not just opinions.[3] The top question surveyed by Dr. Hobbs that is pertinent to this writing:

- What areas of leadership training are requested for pastors to successfully lead a local church-revitalization effort?

One hundred percent of the respondents cited vision as a skill set needed in a revitalization effort. As a pastor coming into a revitalization effort, you must have the vision to see what could be rather than what is. Revitalization is about creatively evaluating

3. The following data is from Paul Hobbs, email sent to seventy-six district superintendents of the Church of the Nazarene, July 15, 2021.

Addition through Subtraction

current resources and how to leverage them to move the spiritual ball down the field to achieve the overall goal, which is reaching more people with the gospel of Christ. Whole books have been written on leading with a vision, so I will not rehash those resources here, but needless to say, you need a vision for the local church, and it starts with your calling. If you know why you are called, you are more likely to understand the how by embracing your calling to help build God's kingdom at your current location.

As respondents were encouraged to list more than one answer, two-thirds of respondents cited prayer or the development of an active prayer ministry as a need in local churches. Revitalizing established churches in many ways is spiritual warfare, and without a strong prayer base, the church will act with continued loss of attendees. Prayer is a central tenet of any revitalization effort. Fifty percent of respondents said that coaching was a missing component of the equation. Reflect on the data that has been gleaned from Dr. Hobbs's research. The top three major issues affecting established churches are lack of vision, lack of prayer, and a lack of coaching. Reviewing the data, if a change does not come through precise training, in church revitalization, the established church will be closing doors more than opening them in the coming years.

Let me wrap up this short chapter by saying that more needs to be done in this arena. The big-C church needs more trained pastors willing to go into the hard places that need help. While the focus has been on church planting for many denominations, one cannot forget or neglect established churches that still have more life to give but need support from leaders and pastors to guide them. The task of revitalization is not a zero-sum game; denominations can plant churches and restore sick churches simultaneously.

9

Revitalization Next Steps

WE HAVE SPENT TIME reviewing theory, practical application, and data, but you want and need more if you are like me. Let me be your virtual consultant for free—well, I guess not free, but for the cost of this book. Walk me through your church, as I want to provide you with some quick steps that you can consider and discuss with others. Please know that the process of church revitalization depends on your leadership, the church board's willingness to embrace seeing things with fresh eyes, the congregation's adaptability, and a prayerful spirit. This process can be sped up or slowed down depending on many factors. Do not take this as the be-all and end-all but a consultation in three thousand words or less.

From the Parking Lot to the Pulpit

As I pull into the parking lot, I view the space as if I were a guest. Statistics have shown that within the first six to eleven minutes of a guest arriving at a church, the guest has decided if they are coming back. Let me say that again: in the first fifteen minutes of a visit, the guest chooses whether or not to attend again. Can we all agree how unfair that is! However, the truth is that before a guest hears you preaching and before they listen to one song sung, your

Addition through Subtraction

church may have blown the guest's experience. While you cannot control the outcome, you can provide a guest with an experience that honors God and opens their heart for more Christian fellowship from your members.

Parking Lot

Have you ever driven by a church, and there is either a gate or a chain across the driveway entrance on a non-service day? I am not sure anyone at the church has stopped to think about what that says to a potential guest. For some of you, I have just stepped on your toes. For others, I can already hear you grumbling that it's for the protection of the church property. But, in all reality, it sends a not-so-subtle message that the church only wants "club members" to attend and not the community. Think about it this way: a chain, gate, or fence in society is seen as a barrier, not a welcome mat for the neighborhood to join your fellowship. While this analysis of your facility can seem petty, for non-church members, you are sending the wrong message.

Scanning the parking lot, I am looking for several things. The first is this: What does the parking lot say about the church? Will guests find signs that say, "No skateboarding," "No overnight parking," "Not a turnaround zone"? In succession, you have told me before I exit my car that the church does not like teenagers, that the church does not trust you, and that you should stop using the church property. Maybe your church has had a bad experience, and thus came the signs, but ask yourself: Do signs deter people or do relationships help people? Signage should be welcoming and informational, not confrontational.

Several years ago, when I arrived at my current assignment, I noticed that the parking lot was gravel, there were ruts in some places, and toward the back of the lot, there was more grass than rocks, and it was overgrown. For churchgoers, we get accustomed to the ripped carpet with duct tape placed over the spot, no signage to provide directions, and, in this case, a parking lot that was not well maintained. With that outlook in mind, ensure that the lawn and bushes are trimmed, the building does not have peeling paint, and the directional signs are unmistakable.

As guests exit the car, they are already unsure of what to do and where to go, so help make it easy for them. In well-established churches, there are multiple entryways, but first-time guests only see doors as barriers to where they want to go. Make sure the main door is marked either with a sandwich sign or a large-letter sign that can be seen long before a guest arrives at the door.

Greet and Direct

Be ready to open the church's doors with a warm smile and helping hand if the guest has children. You probably have heard it said that "a first impression is a lasting impression." Make the first impression of your people and the inside of your building welcoming. Put friendly people at the front door and hide the ones who might be a little sour. Come on; you know who I am talking about in your church—do not think me cross for speaking truth.

When guests enter your foyer, lobby, or narthex, is there someone to guide them to the sanctuary, to show them how to check in their child and where the restrooms are located? Remember: they are visitors and need extra help on their first visit. As I step into your lobby, I am looking around and wondering what decade I have walked into. Sadly, too many entries are stuck in a time warp, or worse—they are decked out as a memorial chapel to the dead. Awards, plaques, memorial rolls, and extensive ornamental flowers need to be removed or scaled back. You need to ask: Do I want to serve coffee and breakfast items in this area or offer a clean space for people to gather? Either way, people want a place where they can talk and interact. By removing the items that are nonessential to a dedicated space like outside the church office, you can create a seating area where people can gather.

Before we move on from this area, let us examine signs again. Are there clear directional signs for me to follow? In my local church, we have put up plexiglass the size of a large sheet of paper (eight by eleven) in strategic locations, and we slide printed signs into them. Every six months, we change these signs, with fresh colors, themes, etc., which saves a considerable amount of money and provides an extra freshness to the facility. So, what about your signage? Make sure that signage is clear, concise, and readable from a distance. As I examine things around your lobby, let me encourage you to remove any unwanted signs that distract from your mission of friendliness. Let me give you two examples. I recently was in a church, and as I came to a side door, it had—not one, not two—but *three* signs taped to the double doors that said, "Make sure the door is closed by pushing on the door." These signs made me smile, because it was clear someone had left the door open before. I went back downstairs to the fellowship hall and recounted my story, and one lovely lady said, "We had four signs, so I guess one fell off." It took all I had not to laugh. Hear my heart: signs will not deter someone from doing what they want, but they will send a message that you might not intend.

The second sign concern is signage that tells me something negative: "Do not bring food or drink into the sanctuary." "Do not open this door." "Water fountain broken; do not use." "Bathroom out of order." These unfavorable signs send a subtle message of negativity when all the church is trying to do is to provide direction. Pay attention to the subtle negative messages sent through signage. Better yet, take down these types of signs.

Care about Children

In many established churches, they desperately want and desire children with families to attend the church. Children bring renewal, hope, and excitement to the facility. As a dad of a six-year-old, I am looking to see if he would be happy in your facility. In my first church, they had to clean out a classroom for my daughters when they were growing up, and if I were not the pastor, I would not have returned. If you want children, prepare now. You might not have a lot of money, but do you have some elbow grease? Clean the toys, throw away broken ones, paint the walls, hang happy pictures, and clean out the classroom. Remember, less is more. You would be surprised at how many times I have walked into churches and seen stained ceiling tiles with mold, sheets on the cribs that looked stained, outdated toys that were hazardous, and stained carpets.

Once you clean up, be prepared with a teacher and curriculum each week, even if you have not had a child for years. Because one day, a child will come, and the parents do not want to see you running around trying to get things together. That certainly will not be a vote of confidence. Part of being prepared is not using outdated material. When a church is struggling, the last thing they can afford is to waste funds, but you need to spend money in this area to keep families with children. Be prepared to have projects and resources that connect with children today.

Retro Restrooms

A pastor was touring me around his church and took me under the main stairwell to the restrooms. The building was over one hundred years old, and the bathroom looked like it had been remodeled in the 1950s. Many of the men's restroom urinals were blocked off by tape, and the remaining ones had no divider between them. I explained to the pastor as a guest that men want their personal space. A simple fix is to put up a partition. The pastor laughed, but I was being serious. We used the plexiglass-sign concept in my local church and placed them at eye level in the men's restrooms. Each week, we slide the Sunday front page, sports section, and comics in them, so that a person has something to review so they do not feel awkward. It is a small gesture to make a guest comfortable.

In the women's restroom, do they have a private area to breastfeed a child and a diaper-changing area that is clean and fully supplied? By the way, a changing station should also be in the men's restroom, and the changing cover could even be camouflage or sports themed to make it more manly, if you want. How about ladies' toiletries? Is there a trash can with a lid so things can be more discreet? I know it may seem silly to go into detail on your bathroom,

Addition through Subtraction

but unsafe childcare areas and dirty bathrooms are two of the things that most turn away guests, according to Thom Rainer.[1]

Worship Center

I made it to your worship center. I scan the space for a safe space to sit. I navigate the seats in the back. I am trying not to sit where a Bible, pillow, or blanket has been left from the week before. Why? Because clearly, someone has marked their territory, and I do not want to be fussed at my very first Sunday with you. Finally, I find a place to sit and begin to scan the room. As I wait, I review the bulletin and then items in the seat pouch in front of me. These three areas will tell me a lot about you. I watch the room to see who is talking or not, who is interested in what, and if anyone will be welcoming to a first-time guest. I look at the pouch in front of me; usually, I find offering envelopes, connection cards, and, a lot of times, old bulletins and candy wrappers. Instantly, it tells me two things: a lack of attention to detail and that the church is struggling to find volunteers to clean up in between services. Petty, you might say, but I say to prepare for guests as if Jesus is coming this Sunday.

The "Special" Music

Whatever the style of music in your church, make sure it is quality. I cannot count how many services I have sat in when a "special" was announced and the person said, "Pray for me. I have not been able to practice this week." I wanted to yell, "*Sit down*! Come back when you are prepared!" I feel God deserves our best, not second, third, or fourth best. Be prepared to shine for God. I did not say you must sing on key—that would be nice, by the way—but you do have to be prepared. Honor God by putting in the time to use your talent for him.

---

1. Rainer, "Top Ten Ways," paras. 6, 13.

Short and Sweet Announcements

My wife was watching a service online recently and said this person spoke for nearly twelve minutes. I said, "Well, that was a short sermon." She replied that it was just announcements. Lord Jesus, take the wheel—or, in this case, take away the microphone. Revitalizer, keep it short and to the point. If a guest is given a bulletin and they can review the announcements on a screen and see them posted on the church's social media page, does someone have to read all the announcements? I think not. Announcements should be secondary, not the main event. However, announcements have become a production instead of a precursor of what is to come. Lessen your announcements to a minimum, or you are wasting your guest's valuable time.

Sermon Preparation

God has called you to bring a message sometimes several times a week to your people, so do not steal someone else's sermons. This should be obvious, but a prominent denomination just had a scandal over pastors liberally borrowing significant passages of text or the whole text. I get it—you're busy. You might be bi-vocational or co-vocational, but if God has called you, let him speak through you when sharing his word, or at least say that it is someone else's sermon and cite it.

As you preach the word of God, make sure it is relevant to your context. Share stories and points that draw your people back to God's word and the direction for their life. Using stories or facts about city life as examples when you live in rural America will only cause disconnection rather than the deep connection you are aiming for. Your style may be different than mine or the pastor down the street, and that is okay. Give yourself permission to preach and teach your way through God's divine calling. But do it relationally. Make the Bible come alive for your guests so they want to know and learn more from God's word.

Addition through Subtraction

Thanks for the Memories

As I leave your service, I am waiting to see if anyone comes over to me to thank me for coming. Think about it this way; this is the last time your church gets to connect with a guest. Sometimes, guests slip out when the pastor is praying, but make sure you love them out the door if they remain. Ask yourself: Have we gotten their information? Were they given an informational card to fill out as they came in? Do they get a gift if they turn it back in? While I could go into great detail on these points, I will save that for another visit; I want to make sure you provide a lasting positive impression for this first-time guest.

As the guest walks back to their car, reflect on what you did right and what you might want to change. For me, as your first-time guest, you did great. While some areas need to be improved or enhanced, your church is on the right track.

Assessments Are *Not* the Be-All and End-All

Assessments are snapshots on a particular day in a specific year. I understand that it was just one service and that usually, you probably do all the things I am questioning better, but people were out or someone forgot to clean. I know that, because I am in the same life-saving business you are in as a pastor. But your guests either may not know or frankly, they might not care. But God does. God cares about your church. God cares about the people currently a part of the church or those who might visit her. Be prepared for guests by doing your best. You may not have the workforce or financial resources to solve all the church's problems, but you can do something. Use this simple consultation for the first time to examine what your church can do better. While you most likely will need a more detailed and specialized assessment, use this as your first step to begin the conversation with your church board and lay members on how to be better prepared for the guests who will attend in the future.

Revitalization Next Steps

Let me close by saying you are doing a lot of things right. You have a remarkable church, and it clearly shows that you love the Lord. However, little things add up. Addition through subtraction is all about taking away the things that no longer fully honor God or the local church in the season your church is in today. Do your church a favor; give a little to gain a lot.

10

Revitalize Your Church: Revitalization Efforts

THE MAJESTIC POLLARD BAPTIST Church stood as a beacon of hope for 126 years, serving the families and neighborhoods around the church. She had withstood two world wars, depressions, and recessions, but she was closing her doors with less than six active members on her rolls. In years past, she had swelled to well over 1,500 members in her heyday, but her death would mark the end of her vaunted life. What happened to Pollard is happening to thousands of churches each year. Pollard refused to change and adapt to the changes around her foundation. When she and other churches like her realized that death was knocking at the front door, death had already overtaken them.

In the early years, Pollard used the technology that was coming of age, the radio, to great effectiveness. The radio became an active evangelism tool, as the pastor's Sunday-night service was carried live over the airwaves to reach thousands with the gospel. It is a reminder that God has a tool for the church to use to contact people with the gospel for every season in her life if she will use it. With each passing Sunday, more and more people came to see in person the man who was striking a chord in their hearts with the gospel of Christ. For twenty-one years, the church seemed to double in size every few years. With each passing year, the pastor became bolder in his preaching style against the sins of society. Instead of scaring away people, the people felt the conviction of his preaching and submitted to Christ at the altars. The church would plant other churches in the community, as their local campus could not handle the size of the crowds that were coming each week. While most members embraced the preaching, a group of board members began plotting to remove the pastor from the church. After twenty-one years of service and tremendous sustained growth, the pastor was voted out by the church board. Local lore says that each board member who voted out the pastor would die within the next twelve-month period.[1]

Church members who remained until the doors closed for good marked that day as the day the church began to decline. Over the following decade, members would start leaving the church, while another group broke off and formed a new church less than two miles down the road. Yet, through it all, the entrenched power inside the church did not change the way they served the community, as they were stuck remembering the good ole days. Sadly, there was a mindset that if the church opened the doors, people would come. Slowly, over time, fewer people went when the doors were open. Sure, there were positive years of increased numbers, but more negative ones came to light over time throughout the decades. The neighborhood around the church began to change. Middle-class families who derived their income from the steel mills in town moved away as the factories relocated or closed. Families who remained became disconnected from the church, as they felt less welcomed as low-income families and a housing project moved into the neighborhood. Instead of adapting to the changing demographics of the community, the church retreated inward.

Three decades ago, the church had another opportunity to change, and they once again chose the status quo. The church board tried to nominate a young pastor, and his mindset of change was too much for those attending for decades. The older generation,

1. Maynard, "End of an Era," para. 20.

Addition through Subtraction

who had lived through the church's heyday, pushed back, refusing to change. A concerted effort formed to vote down his nomination. Small groups of people who disagreed with the board's decision called or visited former members whose names remained on the church membership roll but who had not been attending, in some cases for years, asking them to vote in the church election. The malcontents came out by force, and the pastor was voted down. In the newspaper account of the story by Mark Maynard, for *Kentucky Today*, it was reported that the pastor went on to have success in the next church.[2]

Stop and think for a moment. What would have happened if the pastor had not been voted down? Could the church have grown? We will never know, but we know that death came to Pollard because they made emotional and not data-driven decisions. The story of Pollard could be your story if the church you are leading is not willing to change. Stories like Pollard will become more common if church leadership does not do the hard things to find God's direction for your church.[3]

Warning: Revitalization Needs Revitalizing

Studies have shown that, on average, over four thousand churches close each year, and many more are struggling to hang on. The pandemic has accelerated the deaths of struggling churches. The churches that were already experiencing a turnaround have faced stronger headwinds that have either slowed progress or stopped it altogether. So, how can a church and her leadership know that it is time to revive the revitalization efforts in the local church?

---

2. Maynard, "End of an Era," para. 34.

3. The story of Pollard Baptist Church is taken from Maynard, "End of an Era," and personal conversations with Dr. Matt Shamblin and Pastor J. W. Dunbar.

Warning Sign Number 1: There Is an Absence of a Vision for Kingdom Advancement

The pandemic exposed the heart of churches for their communities. There have been churches that have advanced the kingdom by expanding or adding programs to help feed their neighbors and provide childcare. Still, many others went into a protective bubble, effectively closing off outreach to the community around them. While the virus caused many unknown concerns, the cost to the local church was even more damaging. Churches have tended to focus inward, and it has hindered the advancement of the forward momentum won in the initial battles of the revitalization effort. The focus is now not on the health of the community but the health of the local church. Programs and people-focused outcomes become about serving self rather than serving the community around the church. The heart of living on mission and helping others has waned and, in some cases, stopped altogether.

Warning Sign Number 2: Spiritual Depth and Discipleship Are Lacking

The rate of decline in church attendance has quickened rather than slowed due to the pandemic. According to the Institute of Family Studies (IFS), 34 percent of Americans went to some kind of religious service at least one or two times every month. In 2020, that number dropped to 31 percent and in 2021, 28 percent.[4] Two leading indicators of decay are the lack of spiritual growth and the lack of discipleship within the church. While the church turned inward to focus on their issues early in the pandemic, many have not budged from that posture. Making Christlike disciples out of others, including those around the church, has not happened. This lack of spiritual awareness is causing the church to become stunted in spiritual growth, which will in years ahead harm the church. The lack of spiritual depth and disciple making could show up

---

4. Earls, "Church Attendance Trends," para. 5. See also Hill, "Church Decline and Recovery."

in the absence of new leaders, a lack of volunteers wanting to get involved, a lack of people who invite others to church, and a lack of interest in participating in outreach events that will deplete the spiritual bench for future endeavors.

Warning Sign Number 3: The Congregation Is Dysfunctional

Stress has been heightened for families and many churches as the pandemic has placed under a microscope the fault lines hidden just under the surface of a "normal" Sunday service. In the worst of times, stress causes people to react in an ungodly and harmful fashion. In the best of times, it is a reminder that a person must step back and sometimes step out of the leadership role to focus on self-healing. For many, the church has hidden her faults behind programs and prominent personalities. The hidden dysfunction has now been exposed and is causing great division within the church because of a lack of human resources and because of programs not returning to normal. Revitalization is already not easy, but when you add the stress of change to the focus of life outside the church, the reality is that dysfunction takes over. Dysfunction creates a "me" culture and not a "we" culture, and nothing seems to get done. The established church appears to never come back to her former greatness unless complete surrender is made by all involved.

Warning Sign Number 4: Leadership Seems Inadequate

The pandemic exposed not only dysfunction in the church but also a lack of depth in leadership. Churches have relied far too much on programs and people to propel them forward, but many church members chose not to come back when the pandemic shut down the church. Churches that were once filled are struggling to attain 50 to 75 percent capacity. The worth that leaders found in pews has been deflated by the reality that they preach to far fewer people than twenty-four months ago. The fact is that leadership has now seen they have to do more with less, which in turn has effected the leaders and, in return, is causing burnout. The "way it's always been done" has forced leaders to evaluate their own heart for ministry and what it means to be a leader during this post-pandemic age. Leadership, for all intents and purposes, was built around theological understanding and not around practical shepherding. The lack of training for practical shepherding hinders the church from adapting quickly to the shifting spiritual landscape that many pastors find themselves in.

These four warning signs are just that—warnings that the church must prepare the local body to fight on multiple fronts simultaneously. Prayer, training, and planning will become hallmarks of a revitalization revival in a post-pandemic culture. The church is on the leading edge of a breakdown today. For the church to be the church in this new reality, they will need to be flexible to adapt to the changing landscape while being nimble enough to be forward-looking in training leaders, reevaluating programs for effectiveness, and saturating the altars with prayer for direction. The days for revitalization have never been easy, but with the right outlook, they can be brighter.

Where Does the Church Go?

Church revitalization is frustratingly hard. Every time you think you are getting momentum, something happens, and you must stop. In the past, I have led four churches through stages of church revitalization as the pastor, and countless others as a coach and consultant. Each church story is unique, so let me encourage you not to compare your account with mine or that of another church. But that does not mean we cannot learn from other people's stories. Much of what I learned is not taught in Bible college but through the school of hard knocks from pastoring local churches, so take it from me—you can lead your church into health.

I want to go back to the story of Pollard Baptist Church and pull out vital points from her death.

Addition through Subtraction

Age Does Not Equal Death

Scores of research have been done on the life cycle of churches. I do not buy into the assumption that church age correlates with death. While I respect the data, I guess I am more optimistic that God can still work. Currently, I pastor a church that is seventy-nine years old, and she is vibrant and filled with young families. Yet, I pastored a forty-five-year-old church that was dying with each member's last breath. The church you serve still has life in it if the church is willing to reexamine everything it does and how it is done for the best interest of future guests and not just current members. Without a future-looking vision, the church will stay stagnant and slowly die. Let me encourage you to begin to dream again. Begin to see what could be rather than what is as you move forward in your revitalization efforts. A typical revitalization effort has incredible highs and lows throughout the transition from death to life. Do not get frustrated and walk away from the process too early, as long as you see fruit coming from the efforts. Pollard died not because of age but because the members did not want to change as they aged. They lost focus on their calling and became stuck in the past glories. Take Pollard's story as a warning, and do not allow that to happen to you.

Decisions Determine the Outcome

It is easy to look back and pinpoint several areas where Pollard made decisions that affected the outcome of their story. When you are in the thick of a revitalization effort, you may make a decision that will come back to haunt the church in the process. I like to make decisions fast; however, in a revitalization process, you must move at a pace just outside the comfort zone of your congregation. It is a balancing act between progressing forward and pausing. If you linger too long, you lose momentum and things go back to how they were. Move too fast, and you blow up the whole process before it begins. My counsel to you is to be wise as you move forward, and to keep talking to everyone during the process. Use your authority from the pulpit, conversations, and social media posts to share positive, forward-looking views of where the church is going. Celebrate small wins as big wins and keep sharing the God stories that are happening through the revitalization efforts.

Learn from Past Mistakes

We all make mistakes. In the high-pressure system of turning around a church, you will make mistakes, but learn from them. Pollard did not learn from the mistakes three decades after forcing out their long-term pastor, as members plotted against a would-be pastor before he even was hired. Learn from the Pollard story and do not make the same mistake twice, because the second time could be fatal to your ministry and church. While the past will not determine the church's outcome, it provides a rich trove of learning opportunities. Know your church's story better than its oldest member. Ask questions, listen, and engage in the history of the church so that you can see the land mines, where they were planted, and how you can deactivate them before a land mine blows up the turnaround process. It is delicate and skillful work, but you have the giftings and tools to accomplish the effort.

Renewed in Time

After Pollard closed, she sat empty for over a year. Her well-worn steps that led into her ornate sanctuary saw the occasional homeless person or some teenagers hanging out after school. But God was not done with her yet. Much like your church, God has another chapter to write. Fifteen years ago, God enabled Gateway Church to be birthed across town in a former power-company building. Since that time, they have grown into a thriving church of well over two hundred people in weekly worship. The majority of the attendees are families under the age of forty.

Gateway Church purchased the former Pollard Church and moved their services into her awaiting pews through a God

Addition through Subtraction

transaction. Where once death permeated the property, today, new life has been birthed. Recently the pastor of Gateway shared with me that they have remolded several classrooms to develop a new youth wing and expanded the nursery for the new families coming. They have a host of remodeling ideas on the board once funds become available. All because they were willing to change. While Pollard died after 126 years, today, a fifteen-year-old church plant is thriving in her space. Why? Is it because one was willing to adapt to the changing culture around them, or was it just spiritual luck? You know the answer already—Gateway built in her DNA the ability to shift with the community.

God has great plans for you and your local church, and he has called you to the pioneering work of church revitalization. I promise there will be days of great challenges and triumphs, but if you keep your chin up and knees down, God will help you turn around his church. Each day, the work you do in the trenches of the revitalization efforts is essential to God and the local community where he called the church to serve in ministry. Be encouraged, church revitalizer; God is not done with you yet.

Bibliography

Bickford, Bob. "The Thinking of a Replanter: Visionary Shepherd, Organizational Awareness, Tactical Patience." *Replant Bootcamp* (podcast), July 8, 2020. Episode 42, 28:02. https://replantbootcamp.com/podcast/ep42/.

Blackwell, Kevin. "Church Health and Pastoral Tenure Longevity." September 27, 2018. https://drkevinblackwell.com/2018/09/27/church-health-and-pastoral-tenure-longevity/.

Earls, Aaron. "5 Current Church Attendance Trends You Need to Know." February 2, 2022. Lifeway research. https://research.lifeway.com/2022/02/02/5-current-church-attendance-trends-you-need-to-know/.

———. "Small Churches Continue Growing—but in Number, Not Size." October 20, 2021. Lifeway research. https://research.lifeway.com/2021/10/20/small-churches-continue-growing-but-in-number-not-size/.

Gunter. Nina. "Good News for the Church." Sermon delivered to the 2013 General Assembly of the Church of the Nazarene, Indianapolis, Indiana, June 21, 2013. https://www.preachersmagazine.org/good-news-for-the-church/.

Hill, Enoch. "Church Decline and Recovery during COVID-19." October 28, 2021. https://churchleaders.com/voices/exchange/408841-church-attendance-decline-recovery-covid.html.

Matulka, Rebecca, and Daniel Wood. "The History of the Light Bulb." Department of Energy. November 22, 2013. https://www.energy.gov/articles/history-light-bulb.

Bibliography

Maynard, Mark. "End of an Era: Once Vibrant Kentucky Church Closing Its Doors." *Kentucky Today*, October 6, 2021. https://www.kentuckytoday.com/downloads/end-of-an-era-once-vibrant-kentucky-church-closing-its-doors/article_cd7f3879-3507-5390-a11a-4602404e0c01.html.

O'Dell, Mike. "Letter: The Toughest Job in America?" *Courier*, February 17, 2015. https://baptistcourier.com/2015/02/letter-toughest-job-america/.

Rainer, Thom S. "Five Stages of a Pastor's Ministry." *Thom S. Rainer* (blog), October 5, 2013. https://archive.thomrainer.com/2013/10/five-stages-of-a-pastors-ministry/.

———. "Top Ten Ways Churches Drive Away First-Time Guests." *Timely Church Questions* (blog), November 1, 2014. https://churchanswers.com/blog/top-ten-ways-churches-drive-away-first-time-guests/.

www.ingramcontent.com/pod-product-compliance
Lightning Source LLC
Chambersburg PA
CBHW070514090426
42735CB00012B/2784